For Michael

To one of the greats
of all Time —
With best wishes to you. And
congratulations on your
fine book,

Benjamin Zucker —

HOW TO INVEST
IN GEMS

HOW TO INVEST IN GEMS:

Everyone's Guide to Buying Rubies, Sapphires, Emeralds, and Diamonds

BENJAMIN ZUCKER

Quadrangle / The New York Times Book Co.

I dedicate this book to my three wonderful friends
whom I love—
CHARLES ZUCKER
LOTTY ZUCKER
and
DIANE

Copyright © 1976 by Benjamin Zucker. All rights reserved, including the right to reproduce this book or portions thereof in any form. For information, address: Quadrangle/The New York Times Book Co., 10 East 53 Street, New York, New York 10022. Manufactured in the United States of America. Published simultaneously in Canada by Fitzhenry & Whiteside, Ltd., Toronto.

Book design: Tere LoPrete

Library of Congress Cataloging in Publication Data

Zucker, Benjamin, 1940–
  How to invest in gems.

  Bibliography: p.
  Includes index.
  1. Gems as an investment. I. Title.
NK5530.Z8   332.6'78   75-36261
ISBN 0-8129-0606-3

Contents

	Introduction: Gems—An Excellent Contemporary Investment	vii
I.	Why Gems Today?	3
II.	What Is a Gem?	9
III.	How to Invest in Rubies	13
IV.	How to Invest in Sapphires	26
V.	How to Invest in Emeralds	32
VI.	Comparative Prices of Rubies, Sapphires, and Emeralds in the Past Seven Years	40
VII.	How to Invest in Diamonds	42
VIII.	The De Beers Diamond Syndicate and How It Stabilizes Prices	46
IX.	Other Gemstones	67
X.	Gem Appraisals for Owners and Estate Trustees	69
XI.	What You Can Learn from Auctions	71
XII.	Investment Portfolio: Gems for $5,000, $20,000, $100,000, and $1,000,000	74

Appendix	1. Current Prices of Rubies, Sapphires, Emeralds, and Diamonds	79
	2. Learning about Gems—A Visit to Gem Museums	83
	3. The Gemological Institute of America	90

4. The Evolution of Jewelry and Cutting Techniques 94
5. The History of Fabergé: The Ultimate Craftsman 100
6. Two Men Who Preferred Gems to Paper Money and the Stock Market: Marco Polo and Louis XIV 102

Glossary 109
Bibliography 111
Acknowledgments 115
Index 117

(Illustrations follow pages 8, 40, 50, 72)

Introduction: Gems—An Excellent Contemporary Investment

Precious gems are an excellent area of investment today for anyone with $5,000 or more. Unlike stocks and bonds, which are sensitive to the volume and flow of paper money and have generally decreased in value during our current inflation, the value of colored stones and diamonds has consistently risen. In fact, the price of rubies, emeralds, sapphires, and diamonds has increased thirtyfold in the period since 1900.

Recently the upswing has been dramatic: a 1 carat Colombian emerald of blue green, green green, or yellow green color purchased for $2,000 in 1970 would sell today at auction for approximately $5,000 to $6,000. A 2–3 carat Siamese ruby bought at the same time appreciated similarly over the past five years. There are many indications that this pattern will continue.

This book is designed to teach you how to invest in rubies, sapphires, emeralds, and diamonds, beginning with as little excess capital as $5,000 and working a gem portfolio into the hundreds of thousands of dollars.

People have invested in precious colored stones and diamonds for thousands of years. In the thirteenth century, Marco Polo, probably the most famous gem dealer of all time, left his native Venice and traveled East to the Tartar and Mongol empires in search of gems. We all know how young Marco delighted the Mongol leader Kubla Khan with his storytelling and was rewarded with Chinese gems of sumptuous turquoise and jade, rubies mined in Burma, and sapphires from Ceylon. In the sixteenth century, King Louis XIV wore rubies, sapphires, and emeralds in the daytime and colorless diamonds at night when their "fire" and brilliance would add magic to his candlelit ballrooms.

Kings and princes, financiers, businessmen, and wealthy people in every age have collected these extremely liquid jewels and jewelry, much as art and antiques, to be traded for other goods or resold, to individuals, stores, and at auction. Previously, precious stones were thought to be the province of the very rich, but today a person with $5,000 to $10,000 can purchase selected small stones that may realize a nice profit if held for a number of years.

The step-by-step program outlined here should provide the prospective investor with the background and practical information needed for making wise and enjoyable investments. As with other types of investments, the more knowledgeable you are, the greater are your chances of success. In preparation for sound gem investment, you should plan to visit the gem collections at museums and attend auctions of fine jewelry to train your eye to recognize good quality stones and to record their current market value. It is helpful to find an expert "guide" whom you can trust. It is useful to know how gems are mined and how business is conducted on a "typical day" in the world's diamond syndicate. All of these points are discussed in the following pages.

The core of the book, however, will be the gems themselves: how to evaluate their quality and worth; the mechanics of buying them, including how to talk knowledgeably to a gem retailer and help him to help you; when to resell (gems are a long-term investment). I have planned gem-investment portfolios for those of you with $5,000 $20,000, and $100,000 with some recommendations on the sizes and types of gems to buy. Finally, I discuss the less precious stones that have also proven to be good investments. These cost much less than the precious variety and are newcomers to the gem world. They, too, are worth considering. I recommend that 10 to 20 percent of your assets be invested in gems.

HOW TO INVEST
IN GEMS

I

Why Gems Today?

Historically, precious stones and other "real" items such as gold and silver coins were the primary means of payment for goods and services. When Marco Polo had spent some time with Kubla Khan, he was amazed to discover that the Mongols had developed the first paper currency; a scrap of rice paper printed with rudimentary block letters and countersigned by six Mongol generals. The punishment for counterfeiting was death. The volume of paper currency was quite large and it was accepted throughout the empire.

Marco Polo himself preferred to barter gold for gems and gems for gems. That a man would turn over rare, irreplaceable gems for man-made rice paper seemed preposterous to him. His fears for the stability of such a system were justified several hundred years later when China entered a runaway inflationary period. Paper currency was discontinued by the Ming Dynasty in the fifteenth century.

Likewise, Louis XIV was astounded at the idea of replacing colored stones, diamonds, and silver and gold coins with paper money. Late in Louis's reign, John Law, a Scotsman who had studied finance in Amsterdam and gambling in Venice, proposed to the king that he issue paper currency. Louis refused. But after his death, the new government of France, headed by the Duke of Orleans, adopted Law's suggestion. France prospered and John Law became the most influential economist of his time.

Gem traveler Jean Baptiste Tavernier, who traveled from France to India six times in the seventeenth century. He was the gem buyer for Louis XIV of France.

Why Gems Today? 5

However, the French government secretly began to print vast amounts of paper. Gradually a discount was established between the worth of paper money and gold and silver coinage. At this point John Law formulated his second great innovation—a flotation of a huge stock issue. With the Court's approval he issued stock in a new company called the Mississippi Company. This company had all rights to develop the vast Louisiana territory and parts of India and the Far East.

John Law had engravings printed showing the cliffs of Louisiana covered with emeralds! People were anxious to get rid of their devalued paper money and they used it to buy shares of the Mississippi Company stock, which sold at 400 French livres. Within three years, the stock rose to 18,000 livres. In the meantime, the French government printed and loaned increasing amounts of money to sustain and fuel this speculation. Prices for food, rent, and clothing increased astronomically. Paper money again started to sell at a discount to gold and silver coinage. Suddenly the stock market began to weaken, and within a year it completely collapsed. John Law fled to Venice and died penniless. Throughout this monumental collapse of the French economy, silver and gold coinage maintained its value—as did ruby, sapphire, emerald, and diamond jewelry.

The Uncertainty and Declining Value of Paper Money: The Decline of the Stock Market

The fact that precious gems have risen in value almost every year—even during periods of inflation and deflation—is of crucial importance to you, the potential investor. While we cannot reinstate the barter system of the past and replace gems for paper money, we can accept the reality that our money is buying less and less today, and that this inflationary spiral is likely to continue.

Let's take a simple example. In capitalistic countries not long ago, a man might work most of his life, be able to put a small sum of money in the bank each month, and have a sizable nest egg for his retirement. Today, the situation has dramatically changed. Inflation has become so pronounced that savings (money in the bank) are hardly able to keep up with it. Faced with this, a man might decide to divide his money between savings banks and common stock. A computer study prepared by a midwestern business school revealed that during the period 1925–70, in spite of the 1929–40 depression, an investment in common stock would have put the average investor well ahead of the inflationary pattern of those years, and would have left him with a compounded real annual yield of about 8 percent. However, in the last few years the market has substantially declined, both in the United States and the rest of the world. Consequently, these statisitcs now would be much less favorable.

The recent oil crisis has intensified the international monetary crisis. Arab and Irani leaders have long maintained that because of inflation the oil they were selling to the rest of the world was worth considerably more than the paper dollars they were getting for it. After organizing a cartel of producers, they were able to raise the price from $2 to $10–$12 a barrel. This resulted in the unprecedented transfer of $80–$100 billion from the West to the Middle East.

The money was passed in the form of paper currency (checks, primarily). Thus the Middle Eastern countries are now in a position similar to the aging citizen who wants to provide for his old age. They suddenly have the opportunity to invest on a huge scale, but they don't know exactly where or how to dispose of their money.

At first, the money was left on an overnight basis in banks at home and abroad. Withdrawal could be made on twenty-four hours' notice. The Arabs distrust the stock markets because of the irregularities they have seen and the difficulty of understanding the true worth of each share of stock. They have bought shares of small, quality-producing companies such as Mercedes-Benz and a real estate company in London.

It is my guess that eventually their investments will be scattered, resulting in a percentage in real estate, a percentage in undeveloped land, a percentage in shares of publicly traded companies, as well as a percentage in gold, precious stones, and art objects. In other words, no single possibility would seem to offer the absolute solution, so that a balanced approach of, say, 20 percent in real estate, 20 percent in publicly traded company shares, 20 percent in foreign government bonds guaranteed by those governments, 20 percent in gold and precious stones, and 20 percent in currency holdings would seem to be the best long-term investment. This applies, of course, to the money left over after their own domestic capital needs are met.

On the other side of the coin, the West has had to pay for the $80–$100 billion outflow. There are two ways for Western governments to pay such a massive bill. One is to consume less at home and increase taxes, which would, in effect, save money that needs to be sent abroad for oil. However, this would result in a reduction in the standard of living in Western society.

The other method is simpler: print more paper currency, give it to the Arabs, and hope for the best. While it seems incredible that we would—that all Western countries would—follow such a course, this in fact is what happened in 1974 and 1975. The reserve assets—the amounts of currency and gold in the European and American national accounts—did not decline during 1975. Obviously, the money sent abroad was basically newly printed currency. Or, to put it somewhat differently, the American government printed up large amounts of new currency, let it flow through the system, and a good deal of this extra cash happened to find its way abroad to the oil kingdoms. Fifty billion dollars of new paper money was thus created.

Since prices of goods are related to the volume of currency, what happened in 1975 caused a 10 to 30 percent increase in prices among the Western nations. It is also to be noted that, in general, prices of gems and art objects increased substantially.

The Future: What Will Happen to Money?

It would seem that the long-range prognosis for the economies of the world would include a continuing inflationary spiral, tempered occasionally by sharp deflationary periods where prices will suddenly drop due to unemployment, overproduction, or lack of bank credit (illiquidity). These deflationary periods will tend to be short-lived, and the basic long-term trend of the economies will be inflationary in character. Increasingly more money will move around the world. Because of computers and the latest communications devices, the velocity of money—how quickly it moves between banks, institutions, and governments—will increase (there may be an hourly interest rate instead of a daily interest rate in our not-too-distant future). The system will also become more fragile, and if a mistake is made, it will be made on a vast scale and very swiftly.

Summary

Gems through the ages have enjoyed a "real" value that is not possible with paper money and stocks, which are more volatile. Gems are also highly liquid and can be converted into cash quickly and with relative ease. Finally, gems are easily transportable (witness refugees fleeing during the past wars, who sewed rubies and diamonds into the hems of their clothes and sold them at a profit when they arrived in a safe haven). A ring or necklace containing a precious stone may be worn for pleasure and sold, in five years, at a price that often far exceeds what was originally paid for it.

These four rubies, gem quality, are 3–7 carat sizes. The upper left cushion shape is from Burma. The upper right oval shape and the square shape are more purple and are from Thailand. The small, pinkish, lower right stone is from Ceylon.

Photograph by John Cubito

The Burmese variety, purer red, is the top ruby color. As the red color contains more orange, more purple, or more pink, the price declines.

Photograph by Reid Rutherford

Above Thai ruby, square cut. Practically flawless internally.
Photograph by John Cubito

Below Luminescent view of ruby—oval shape, most common in rubies. 10 carat size. Can be worth $15,000 per carat.
Photograph by Reid Rutherford

Above These are ruby melee or small faceted stones, the size of a letter on this page (3 mm.). These stones can wholesale for $4 to $10 apiece, in commercial Thai quality.
Below Closeup of ruby melee. It is amazing how a human can put fifty-eight facets on a stone all by hand.

Photographs by Milton Moses Ginsberg

The range of color in sapphires. Note the violet, gray, green, and cornflower shades of blue.

Photograph by Reid Rutherford

The Star of India, on display at the American Museum of Natural History, New York City, is the large, grayish blue star sapphire. The deep blue sapphire to the right (gem top quality color) is from Burma (on loan from Precious Stones Company, New York). On the left is a star ruby, and on the bottom, the brownish, midnight-star sapphire.

Photograph by Dr. Vincent Manson

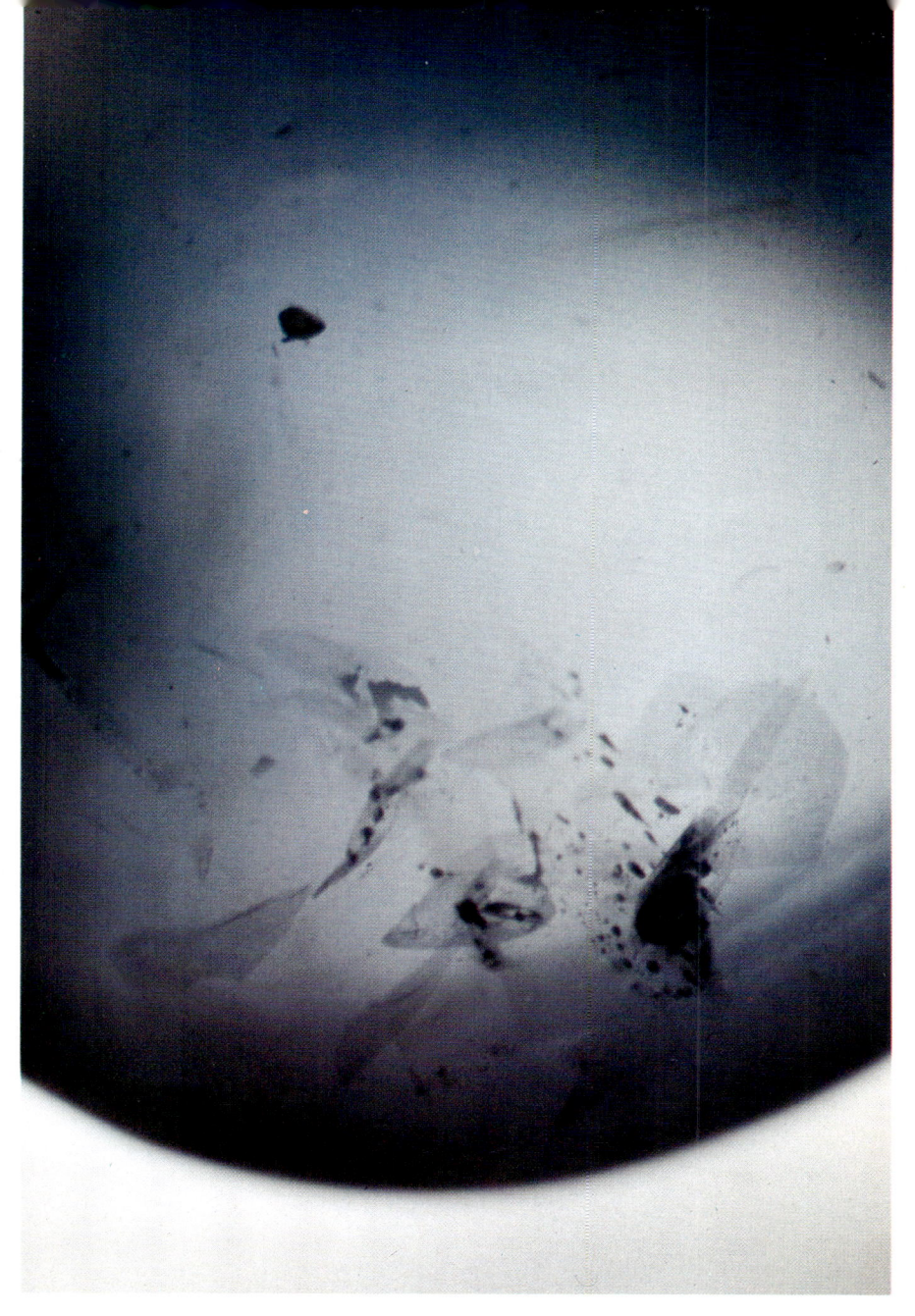

The black dotlike substances are zircon crystals imbedded within the sapphire. This photo was taken in a microscope and is a 100 times magnification. Because the zircon crystal does not have a color halo around it, the stone is presumed to have come from Burma. This is a detail of the Precious Stones Company's sapphire now at the Museum of Natural History.

Photograph by Dr. Vincent Manson

This extraordinary 94 carat Kashmir-color, fine blue star sapphire is on display at the American Museum of Natural History, on loan from the Precious Stones Company, New York.

Photograph by John Cubito

II

What Is a Gem?

In every culture throughout civilized man's history, men and women have adorned themselves with bracelets, necklaces, amulets, seals, and other forms of jewelry. Today all cultures in our world wear jewelry.

A Masai herdsman going into the fields in East Africa may carry a walking stick and wear a simple cotton robe, but his neck and arms are bedecked with bright bead bracelets and a red bead necklace. In one respect, he is little different from the guitar-playing eighteen-year-old girl in California, who wears a whole series of intertwined silver necklaces and turquoise rings, or from the fashionable French doctor's wife with her delicate red ruby ring.

The reasons for this fascination with gems are many, encompassing psychology and magic. I will treat this extensive subject very briefly in the following pages.

A Gem's Shape

In her book, *The Universal Bead* (New York: W. W. Norton, 1969), Joan Erickson posits an interesting theory about gems which relates primarily to their shape. Dr. Erickson notes that many primitive societies, among them the Eskimos, African tribesmen, and American Indians, have used beads as currency. The beads were relatively rare and

Eye beads. In all bead-wearing societies, the beads with dots on them, resembling eyes, are the most sought-after. There is a connection between beads, gems, and a mother's eyes. Photo courtesy of W.W. Norton, New York, from *The Universal Bead* by Joan Erickson, 1969.

therefore served as an effective method of valuation. In many cultures, the most highly prized bead was one with a dot in the center, which was called the "eye bead" because it looked like a human eye. In fact, the Chinese character for the pupil of the eye is the same as the character for bead.

Dr. Erickson refers to psychological experiments showing that when a child is very young, one of his first means of contact with his mother and father is through their eyes. If a parent looks away, the child will begin to cry. Other experiments show that a circular mask with painted eyes, but without a nose or mouth, will elicit a smile and a favorable response from a very young infant. On a deep psychological level, therefore, gems may represent a reflection of the parents' eyes.

This could provide an answer to those people like myself who have wondered why the Indians sold Manhattan for a mere $24 worth of beads. On an existential level, the beads

What Is a Gem?

had a value to the Indians that far surpassed the value of Manhattan Island, beautiful as it must have been in those days.

Beads = Gems = A Mother's Eyes

This eye–bead–gem is therefore a symbol of contact between the individual and the outside world. One would expect, in various art forms, to find this shape used to symbolize reassurance or the search for reassurance. Van Gogh's portraits, for example, reveal the luminescent qualities of the eyes. Toward the end of his life, van Gogh painted at terrific speed—nearly one painting a day—and his finest masterpieces, such as "The Starry Night" or "Wheat Field and Cypress Trees," have a circular bead pattern repeated endlessly in the sky. The sun, the moon, and the starry night appear simultaneously, and one can almost see the universe in van Gogh's mind dissolving back into this primitive, circular, beadlike gem pattern. A gem is the center of the world.

A Gem's Color

The color of a ruby, emerald, or sapphire is most important, both as an indicator of its value in the marketplace and with regard to psychological preference and status. There are literally thousands of shades of red, blue, and green. Each stone you are considering buying should be judged according to what shade and color you personally like and what that color stone might command when you decide to sell it.

In the Middle Ages, the color blue was identified with heaven, the sky, and life after death. Blue sapphires were sought as jewels for the church hierarchy. Bishops always wore them.

Red, in most cultures, conveys feelings of vibrancy, excitement, and passion, as it is the color of blood. Green, with its basic vegetationlike shades, carries an organic feeling and is usually regarded as soothing and optimistic.

With diamonds, it is the absence of color, the perfect whiteness, that makes it a "good color." The pure white color was the focal point of Herman Melville's *Moby Dick*, where the whiteness of the whale made it an otherworldly symbol of perfection. That which is white would seem to endure forever, and combined with the hardness of the diamond material, the stone has the underlying symbolism and reality of durability.

A Gem's Internal Brilliance

A gem contains an inner light that can be accentuated by careful faceting or cutting. The fact that the stone has this ability to sparkle when it is turned endows it with a magical property. At one time, each type of stone was said to have magical powers against specific illnesses or evils and the wearers of certain stones were regarded as especially powerful. A ruby would be ground up and used as an antidote for heart trouble; sapphire powder in liquid would cure headaches.

Therefore, whether one considers the shape, color, or brilliance of a stone as the source of its appeal, one is left with a feeling that there are deep-seated reasons why generation after generation has treasured the wearing of stones.

III

How to Invest in Rubies

The Bible contains frequent references to rubies, such as "Who can find a virtuous woman, for her price is far above rubies?" (Proverbs 31:10)

A ruby is a red variety of aluminum oxide. The red variety of this mineral, which is called corundum, is caused by minute traces of chromium. The more chromium, the redder the stone. The ruby tends to grow in crystal form and is part of the hexagonal crystal family. It develops over millions of years under the ground. Sometimes crystals work their way up through the ground because of geological disturbances. They might then be carried by rivers to points far from the original concentration of ruby crystal underground.

Mining for Rubies

Where did the rubies of biblical times come from? Most likely they came from the ruby mines at Mogok, Burma, where the finest shades of rubies are still mined. Ruby mining has always been primitive. The mine is essentially a well, hand dug by a few people, often a family, to a depth of ten to thirty feet. A man is lowered by a rope pulley system to the bottom, where he scrapes up layers of gravel. The gravel is then lifted in buckets to the top of the well. When the day's scraping is finished, the miners sort the gravel for possible ruby crystals.

This system is still used today because it prevents the careless crushing of the valuable ruby crystals found haphazardly imbedded in the rock. Ancient cutting tools have been found at the Mogok mining site, giving archeological proof that mining for "ruby rough," as the uncut crystals are called, has been going on since prehistoric times. The chips of crystal rock are eventually cut and faceted and sold to traveling gem merchants.

Geologists to date have been unable to perfect a system that can detect an underground ruby deposit. Wells are dug in a hit-or-miss fashion wherever ruby crystals are seen on the surface. Sometimes the veins of accompanying minerals are traced and mining is based on an educated guess, but usually this method, too, is doomed to failure (99.9 percent of the time the presence of crystals on the surface signifies nothing).

In the mountainous valley at Mogok and in Ceylon, the people have for many centuries, through exceedingly hard work and at great risk, scraped the surface of the earth and wrested tiny bits and pieces of these beautiful, rough stones.

Mining areas have historically been fairly dangerous places for outsiders. In ancient Burma, for example, miners were required to give the king any ruby rough that would yield a stone greater than six carats. Consequently, many large stones were broken into smaller parts. Burmese mines were excavated clandestinely at night: a dangerous practice, but considered necessary to avoid the king's supervision. Local miners engaged in secretive daytime mining that could be halted at a minute's notice in the event of a visit from royal inspectors.

This pattern of local people mining for themselves and fearing outsiders is common today in Thailand, Brazil, Colombia, Kenya, and other parts of the world. In Colombia, for example, there are bandit miners who carry guns while they mine, and the Colombian government recently had to send in the army to introduce a semblance of law and order.

From the mining areas throughout the world, the rough stones are sent to more civilized, safer trading centers, often far away from the mines, to be cut. The stones are seldom cut at the site of the mine. Gem dealers come to the trading centers to buy the cut and faceted output in large lots.

In Burma today, because the mines are so ancient and have been so carefully worked over, there are very few top-quality pieces of rough left. The situation is further complicated by the Burmese government, which is carefully building a socialist society and opposes freewheeling capitalism. Consequently, there is no active gem center for buying and selling rough in Burma. Nor is there are centralized, well-financed export cartel that might successfully market colored stones on a worldwide basis, as exists in Russia for its diamond output. What does exist is a series of fairly small, frequently undercapitalized colored stone dealers and a highly fragmented, worldwide colored stone market.

So small is the supply of rubies and so close-knit are the dealers that the following anecdote represents a common occurrence: A fairly large retailer placed an advertisement in a New York newspaper to sell a 14 carat ruby, priced at $210,000. This stone was, in fact, recognized by a dealer as one that he had passed up in Bangkok. Another dealer had bought the ruby in Bangkok in partnership with still a third dealer; the latter shipped the stone to New York and had it mounted in a ring at a French jewelry mounting house, which did a lovely job of bringing out the splendid color inherent in the stone. The ruby was then given on a six-month consignment basis to the retailer who advertised the ring.

Even if the stone had been less than 7 carats, it probably would have been recognized as there are so few fine rubies available. One could even give each stone in the market a name! Quite often dealers can recognize the stones, having seen them before in the Far East, Europe, or in New York.

Judging the Color of a Ruby

The color of a ruby and other precious stones is critical in judging origin and market value. In the case of a ruby, the shade is determined by the chromium deposits within the stone. The amount of chromium in a ruby varies to an infinitesimally small degree among mining sites in Ceylon, Burma, Thailand, Cambodia, Afghanistan, and, more recently, Kenya; but it can make all the difference between a $5,000 stone and one of the same size that is worth less. A Thai ruby has often increased in percentage more than a Burma ruby over the past few years.

One of the talents that marks the expert in colored stones is the ability to remember shades of red within rubies and to keep that memory clear and accurate over many years. Because diamonds have been standardized to such a great extent by the Gemological Institute, this color memory for a diamond dealer is no longer as important. He can simply say, "In the early 1970s I sold a 3.22 carat round diamond D-flawless stone for $12,500 a carat." Or, "I sold a 3.22 G-color VVS_1 stone for $3,800 per carat." The color and clarity (flawlessness) grades serve to recall the exact stone for the dealer.

But the colored stone expert must remember, for example, the balance among the blue, violet, and orange shadings within the red ruby. The investor, likewise, must be knowledgeable about the different shades of red that connote a ruby's origin. You can seek advice from a reputable dealer—always a good idea even for those who have trained their eye—but it is important to have a grasp of the essential differences yourself. The following simple chart may help.

Characteristic Colors of Rubies

Burmese Ruby	Finest shade is full-bodied red with a touch of orange in it at the very center of the red spectrum. Called "pigeon's blood" or "Burmese red." A blackish, bluish red stone or one with too strong a hint of pink is of lesser quality.
Ceylon Ruby	More pink variety of red, called "Ceylon red" in gem dealer shorthand.

Siamese Ruby	Slightly violet shade of red, called "Siamese red," and often exceedingly brilliant.
African Ruby	Somewhat brownish shade of red.

Unfortunately, color differentiation isn't always simple. One can sometimes see a Burmese stone that is pink or a fine Ceylon ruby that has a deep red color. There is no doubt that Marco Polo would have called a very pink Burmese ruby a Ceylon ruby. Likewise, a spinel has a peculiar cast of red that is generally unmistakable, a kind of deep, raspberry purplish cast or, more commonly, an orange shade of red.

The Bank Melli in Iran houses some of the world's finest rubies along with many spinels. There is proof that when the original collections were formed over the centuries by the Moghul rulers in Delhi, little differentiation was made between the spinels (a different gem, which crystallizes in a different fashion and is chemically different) and the rubies. If the spinel had less purple and contained a more natural red shade, it was probably considered a ruby. In those times, there was a stone called a "balas" ruby, which was actually a spinel. Only after these gems had been carried off by the Nadir Shah of Persia, and scientific testing of the stones completed some two hundred years later, could the spinels be distinguished from the rubies. The price of a ruby can be one thousand times greater than that of a spinel because of the ruby's greater rarity and beauty. But have no fears for the Irani treasury despite the profusion of spinels. There are many rubies left over for even the rainiest days in Teheran!

Gem dealers and buyers are not always in agreement about the origin of a stone. A dealer might say: "Here is a nice 3 carat Burmese ruby," and the buyer might immediately protest, "That's not Burmese, that's Ceylonese. Can't you see all the pink in that stone?" And because there has been no precise method of measuring the color shades of colored gems, this argument and its variations often lead to zesty disputes.

A fascinating aspect of determining whether a ruby is pink

or red has always been that the color is dependent on the light it is seen in—in a shop window along Fifth Avenue; in a room with an overhead incandescent light; in a broad, outdoor Indian setting; in an overcast Northern natural light; in an Amsterdam gem office. Each of these lights has a distinct effect on how the human eye views the ruby. One of the gem dealer's distinctive talents must be to add or subtract in his mind portions of the color and brilliance that he sees, so he can make allowances for being in Amsterdam, in India, or inside a New York retail establishment with incandescent lighting.

A June afternoon in Bombay, aside from the fact that it may be 110 degrees outdoors, will emit a light so overpoweringly bright that the ruby will take on a magnificent deep red color with a vibrant cast of brilliance. Perhaps this is why gems are so highly prized in India; the sun seems to reveal all the inherent possibilities of the beauty of the light within the gemstone.

If the same stone is shipped to New York and examined in natural New York daylight, it will appear a considerably darker shade of red and less brilliant. This is due to the high amount of pollution over New York and to the fact that New York lies farther from the equator than Bombay. But Amsterdam light is even grayer than New York daylight! And finally, under an incandescent light indoors a ruby will appear to be more brilliant and will sparkle more, but the color might change enough to make the ruby look a bit more purple.

There are two possible solutions to the problem. Socrates said that if a man is wise enough he can sit in his own home in his own chair and wait, and the whole world of knowledge will stream to his doorstep. At the very top of the gem profession today there are men who sit at their desks and examine each stone offered them under their own, never varying lighting conditions. At first I thought these men had become so wealthy that they did not want to face the rigors of traveling to the far corners of the gem world. However, I now see that by standardizing the light they have greatly reduced their chances for unpleasant surprises in the purchase of gems.

The other possibility, however, is the more adventurous one, the riskier one, the one that leads to seeing more gems, the one that Marco Polo used, namely, buying under any light but examining the stone in as many lights as possible within that environment. A gem dealer in Bombay, on that sunny afternoon, would hold the ruby at the window and look at the stone. He would then examine the stone in the shade. He might take it indoors and examine it under artificial light. In general, he would try to play with the ruby at different times of the day—when the sun was more intense, and then less bright—so that he could achieve a balanced idea of how the stone really looked.

As inexact as this seems, it has been employed for generations and is still used today.

What the Inside of Rubies Look Like

Inclusions are one of the most fascinating distinguishing characteristics of the gem. They are tiny growth markings within the colored stone or the diamond. Gems take many millions of years to grow; if there are any unusual occurrences during this long, slow period—for example, if spinel crystals are suddenly interjected into a ruby—the resulting ruby crystal will, under magnification, show a tiny spinel crystal. When the layman sees such a ruby, he will assume that this is simply a flaw or a darkish spot within the stone.

Within rubies or sapphires from Burma one can find elongated, crisscrossing needles of foreign material called "rutile." This rutile is so densely intertwined that if the stone is tilted at a certain angle the markings can sometimes be seen with the naked eye. This is called "silk." If these needles extend virtually through the whole stone, we have a silk that is characteristic of Ceylon rubies or sapphires.

The silk in rubies helps determine whether a stone is from Burma or Ceylon, but there are a host of other inclusions that will point the way to the ruby being of Thai or African origin. Both Thai and African rubies are created under conditions of enormous geologic pressure. Consequently, when these stones are examined under a microscope, parallel lines, which are called "stress lines" or "twinning lines," can often be seen. The material has been subjected to so much pressure that the crystal has actually spun around on its axis repeatedly while growing.

How to Value a Ruby

The primary consideration in determining the value of a ruby is the depth of the redness of the stone. A 1 carat ruby can vary between $50 a carat and $8,000 a carat depending on the shade of red. Each stone differs in its internal landscape—the amount of chromium, the number and length of inclusions—and this can affect redness. The red color is generally not spread uniformly throughout the stone, but is more intense in one section. Rubies are never without inclusions (flawless).

Like other commodities, supply and demand affect the price. Very few new ruby mines have been discovered in the last three thousand years. Aside from the ruby mines discovered recently in Kenya, there have been no mines of any consequence found in the last generation.

The supply of rubies, therefore, which has always been limited, is becoming smaller. It follows that the larger the ruby, the more valuable it will be (provided it is relatively free of inclusions and color deficiencies). Rubies over 5 carats are considered extremely rare.

How to Distinguish Genuine from Synthetic Rubies

Stones that are cut and faceted bend light (refract) as the light passes through them. The denser the atoms are packed within an object the more the light will bend as it hits the material. The amount of bending can actually be measured on a fairly simple instrument called a refractometer, manufactured by the Gemological Institute in California. The instrument ranges between 1.80 on its upper length and 1.45 at the bottom length. The higher the number the more optically dense the material and the higher the "refractive index."

The degree of bending varies from extreme highs, found in diamonds, to low degrees of refractiveness, as in opals. In a highly refractive stone that is cut well one will see a great amount of brilliance. If one were to place a diamond and a ruby next to an emerald, one would immediately see that the emerald, even if well-cut and not greatly flawed, is considerably less brilliant than the diamond. Because emeralds are less densely packed than rubies or diamonds, generations of gem cutters have learned that if they make the bottom part of the stone (the pavilion section) deeper, the stone will often improve somewhat in brilliance.

If a stone is placed on a refractometer, the machine will measure the amount of light bending. If the figure, which is clearly visible on the index, reads 1.77, there is an indication that the stone is a possible corundum; if it is a red stone, as opposed to any other color, it can be called a ruby. Glass, for example, has a different degree of bending and would not register the same figure on a refractometer. Neither would most red garnets. However, interestingly enough, a synthetic ruby would register exactly such a reading on the refractometer. Specific gravity and a microscope would finally confirm corundum and separate a synthetic from a genuine ruby.

The ruby has been sought after for many centuries. Occasionally a stone that resembles a ruby, such as a spinel or garnet, might be mistaken for one and sold at a ruby price to the unwary buyer. Gem testing in the early days was virtually nonexistent. The most common look-alike for a ruby was a spinel; while the two stones can generally be distinguished from each other by a sensitive, trained eye, it is only in our century that one has been able to distinguish *scientifically* between the two red stones. The refractive reading would immediately give a reading of 1.718 for a spinel, a reading much lower than for the more densely packed 1.77 ruby reading.

In ancient times, a great deal of glass was cut and faceted to simulate rubies. Today, a refractometer or a microscope can distinguish between glass and rubies. Around the turn of the century, in Paris, a very impressive tour de force was achieved by Verneuil. He was able to reproduce synthetically a stone that had the same density as a ruby, the same specific gravity, and similar chemical constituents. He set up a tiny spatula onto which slowly fell a powdered mixture of aluminum, oxide, and chromium. This powder passed through a flame before it built up on the spatula. The material which collected on the spatula in the shape of a *boule* looked somewhat like a short-stemmed wine goblet, with the spatula forming the base.

Because Verneuil's gems took only a few weeks to grow, compared with the millions of years that it takes nature to create a ruby, differences do exist that betray these differing growth rates. On a refractometer, the synthetic ruby shows the same reading as a genuine stone. However, under microscopic investigation, the material building up in circular fashion on the spatula and following the curved outside lines of the goblet reveals rounded "growth" lines. In nature, the ruby grows in a six-sided (hexagonal) pattern so that the gem, when viewed under a jeweler's loupe or microscope, will show a straight ground line pattern. A natural ruby also contains many tiny foreign crystals that, of course, are not present in the synthetic gem.

Finally, there is the fluorescence test. A natural ruby placed under an ultraviolet lamp reveals atoms and electrons within the stone that are excited and glow. If the stone is of Burmese origin, it will have a moderate red fluorescence. If it is from Ceylon, the fluorescence will be a bit less pronounced. Most other rubies—Siamese or African—will remain very dark. If you put a synthetic ruby under an ultraviolet machine, the stone will generally turn a vivid red color.

In summary, by submitting your gem to the refractive index test, looking at the stone under fluorescent light, and examining it under a microscope, you can ascertain if it is genuine or synthetic. If any uncertainty remains despite these tests, for about $30 to $35 the Gemological Institute will examine the stone in question and give you a written certificate of authenticity.

Where to Buy Rubies

You might think that the obvious place to buy a ruby, or any precious gem, would be the Far East. The fact is that each step in the miner–cutter–wholesaler–retail dealer journey adds an amount of expertise. It is difficult even for an experienced gem merchant to evaluate the worth of a stone directly from the mine, before it is cut and faceted. The layman would generally be out of his element. Likewise, Chinese gem dealers in Hong Kong or Bangkok do not look favorably on the one-time amateur buyer.

I advise you to purchase your gems from a fine retail establishment, even though you admittedly pay a retail markup. Your retailer should give you a certificate of genuineness on your purchase and can arrange for exchanges or refunds (in some cases). If you establish a good rapport, your relationship can be a mutually profitable one lasting for a good many years. Many dealers and stores are willing to purchase gems from their investor–customers at the market price when you are ready to sell.

A common custom in the precious stones business is for a retail jeweler to act as an adviser to the investor for a fee of 5–10 percent. It is understood that the retail jeweler will aid the investor in making a sound decision. The "guide" is under a fiduciary responsibility to the investor.

Ruby Valuations in Different Currencies

There is yet another yardstick for computing the value of rubies, and that is rubies as opposed to the dollar or other paper currencies. We have already discussed the diminishing purchasing power of American currency since World War II. But what about money in other countries?

Unfortunately, currencies have not moved together. This means that a 1 carat gem ruby may sell for anywhere from $5,000 to $8,000 wholesale today, depending on whether the currency in use is American dollars, German marks, or Kuwaiti dhirams.

Importance of Viewing More Than One Stone

The dealer in colored gems maintains a large inventory of rubies. When he is shown a ruby for appraisal or possible purchase, he compares its color with stones he already has in stock. As an investor, likewise, you should expect to see four or five rubies at the retail store or dealer's showroom before you decide to buy. You owe it to yourself to compare color (one may be too pink), size (too small or too big), and shape. By making these comparisons, you will also sharpen your eye for color and brilliance.

Weight versus Purity of Rubies and Other Precious Stones

In the past, when gem material was more plentiful and cheaper, only the finest grades of inclusion-free materials were used. More recently, second-grade material with various inclusions, color flaws, and other detriments has been faceted and sold to unsophisticated buyers. In addition, a cutter may prefer to get a larger, more imperfect stone—one that will weigh more and probably sell for more money to the uninitiated—than a smaller, more perfect one. Naturally one can recut a stone; but this is relatively rare in the colored stone and diamond fields.

Where to Sell a Ruby and When to Sell It

Selling a ruby, as well as selling any sapphire, emerald, diamond, or other precious stone, should be done by first

How to Invest in Rubies

appraising the stone as to the current market value. After ascertaining the market value, either the stone should be auctioned or sold to a dealer or reliable retailer. An important dealer or retailer is always keen to buy precious stones at wholesale prices. Precious stones are among the very few products for which advertisements to buy (not to sell) exist each day in major newspapers. Important precious stones can always be sold in the wholesale market.

SIGNIFICANT EVALUATIONAL QUESTIONS FOR RUBIES

1. Authenticate it as being corundum and a ruby.
2. Try to ascertain, by looking at the color, which area of the world the stone comes from. Siam and Ceylon rubies (of fine quality) have risen proportionately as much as Burma rubies, although they are generally less expensive per carat.
3. With the aid of gemological instruments, examine the internal properties of the stone and establish more definitely, on the basis of these physical findings, the origin of the stone.
4. Judge the stone in relation to its mounting. Does the mounting do the stone justice? Is the mounting too overpowering for the stone itself? How could the mounting be changed or made to better enhance the stone? Is there a way that the stone itself could be altered to fit the mounting?
5. What is the value of the stone? This is a highly subjective question, especially in the field of rubies. We shall deal with it more fully in the Appraisal section of this book. It is based on how fine the red is, how large the stone is, and, finally, how brilliant and clear the ruby is. No ruby is flawless.
6. Try to obtain a reputable guide who, for a 5–10 percent advisory fee, can aid you in negotiations with the seller of the ruby.

IV

How to Invest in Sapphires

A sapphire is a stone that has the same chemical and physical properties as a ruby. Both are varieties of the corundum family, which is an aluminum oxide compound that crystallizes in the ground over millions of years. All corundum that is not red is considered sapphire, while red corundum is ruby.

Sapphires appear in colors other than blue, including yellow, green, and purple. However, the blue shade has always been considered the most desirable and therefore the most valuable of sapphires.

The blue color of sapphires is caused by an iron impurity within the stone. Differing amounts of iron will give different tints of blue. Sapphires with a greenish tint usually come from Australian rough. Those of a grayish or violet cast are often from Ceylon; those with a royal blue color are from Burma. Sapphires with a fine cornflower velvety blue color are from Kashmir. Thai sapphires range from a very delicate blue to a blackish blue.

Mining and Cutting Sapphires

Ceylon is the major source of sapphire today; Thailand is the second. Principally, the stones are found either in the ground or on the banks of a river. In Ceylon, for example, the rivers carry the sapphire far from the original mine shaft. By sorting out the gravel along riverbanks and washing away extraneous rock, miners can rescue the sapphire crystals.

This process of searching for alluvial gem deposits—deposits carried by a river—is the most ancient of mining processes. Panning for gold, searching for river diamonds, and looking for river sapphires are all somewhat similar techniques. One can spend thousands of hours hoping to recover, perhaps once or twice in a lifetime, a significantly large sapphire crystal. Frequently, the key to finding sapphires is to search where the river used to flow, not in its current location. Over the course of millions of years, geologists believe, rivers that make wide bends have tended to change direction inch by inch. Sapphire crystals may be found in the debris if stones have settled down and formed sedentary rock.

Once a Ceylon panner has collected a goodly supply of sapphire crystals, he passes them along to a merchant who buys from all of the miners at work on the riverbank. The merchant, in turn, takes the crystals to a cutting center. An expert planner looks at each individual crystal, holding it up to the sun to guess what is inside, where the imperfections lie, and how large a stone can be cut from that piece of rough crystal. He might be able to look into the stone only through certain angles; or the rough stone may be completely opaque from the outside and a section of it must be cleaved off for an interior view.

The Ceylon State Gem Corporation has revolutionized the gem business in Ceylon (Sri Lanka). As Mr. Alexander of the corporation explained to my partner, Luzer Kaufman, and to me, each sapphire or ruby now exported from Ceylon is tested so that only genuine stones can leave the country. In addition, many mining surveys are being conducted by the State Gem Corporation. Cutters are being trained and the Ceylon government is actively trying to modernize the sapphire and ruby business with the hope of earning more foreign exchange to speed Ceylon's growth. Worldwide publicity concerning the beauty of Ceylon stones is sent to the major trading areas of precious stones throughout the world. Ceylon has been the largest source of stones to the world for the last three thousand years. It is impressive to see that the government is trying to nationalize its precious stone business and assure its growth in the future.

How to Distinguish Genuine from Synthetic Stones

Because of the high price of sapphires and the great demand for them, there are large amounts of synthetic sapphires being manufactured today. The Gemological Institute has perfected instruments that test the genuineness of sapphires. The process for testing synthetic sapphires is very similar to the testing procedure for synthetic rubies, including the use of the microscope and ultraviolet light to detect the nature of the inclusions and the growth patterns.

Dr. Gubelin, Dr. Schubnel, and several other gemologists have done landmark research on both microscopic and photographic analyses of gemstone inclusions. A Burmese sapphire contains rutile needles that crisscross each other in a densely woven pattern that resembles silk. If the Burmese sapphire is heavily included, the sunlight can often pick up the reflections of the silk so that they may be seen with the naked eye. This silk is certainly apparent under a 10-power jeweler's loupe and even more apparent under a microscope.

Over the millions of years that Burmese sapphires were being formed in the Mogok Valley of Burma, liquidlike inclusions were forming within the stones. Dr. Gubelin has identified a "crumpled flag" type of inclusion: a tiny, fan-shaped liquid inclusion. Amazingly enough, under 100-power magnification this fan will have a serrated edge similar to the folds in a velvet curtain. If this edge is not serrated but simply rounded, it is a sign that the sapphire is from Ceylon. Highly accurate pictures in synthetic shades of color have been taken of these minute inclusions.

Dr. Gubelin has also isolated patterns of inclusions that are common to the Kashmir sapphires from India. Kashmir stones are a fabulous cornflower blue color. However, their liveliness is dulled somewhat by a velvety, foggy texture. With the aid of a microscope, a mass of internal, slender,

How to Invest in Sapphires

capillarylike rutile fragments that pervade the internal world of the Kashmir stone are apparent. Sapphires from Thailand have a large number of included crystals; deposits of minerals that entered the sapphires (zircon, pyrite, rutile, etc.) became trapped there while the stones were crystallizing. Sapphires also come from Yogo Gulch, Montana. They have a distinctive color cast, but more telling is the fact that their included crystals and liquidlike inclusions form a definable unit. Sapphires tend to have fewer inclusions than rubies or emeralds, but the investor should not expect to find a flawless colored stone.

Comparison of Prices of Precious Gems

It is interesting to note the long-term relationship between the prices of rubies, sapphires, emeralds, and diamonds. Rubies and emeralds of fine quality, in sizes above 3 carats, are more valuable than diamonds above 3 carats. Sapphires have a value of generally one-third to one-half less than rubies and emeralds. These ratios have been in existence for three thousand years, subject only to such changes in supply as the opening of diamond mines in Brazil in 1724 (which resulted in a major drop in the price of diamonds).

In this country, a sapphire rough could conceivably be cut in some six to ten hours. But that is like saying a Rembrandt canvas could be painted in an hour of diligent work. The more delicate the desired results, the more human decision and imagination will be required each step of the way.

For the last three thousand years, Ceylon sapphires have been cut with a very deep pavilion, or bottom, to the stone—like cutting an egg in half, with the flat top of the egg as the table of the stone and the rounded part the bottom. This deep portion assures a lot of internal reflection, and Ceylon stones tend to be very lively.

On the minus side, this large bottom half of the stone adds considerable weight to it. Since the gem world quotes prices on a per carat basis, as opposed to a per stone basis, one pays for the extra weight. Dealers derisively refer to such sapphires as having a "Bombay back" and want to pay less per carat. Another frustrating feature of the deep pavilion is that the back of the stone cannot be seen when a Ceylon stone is mounted in a ring. Only the smaller tabletop is visible, giving the sapphire a 10–20 percent smaller appearance than its total weight would indicate.

It is an amusing experience to show a Ceylon sapphire to a diamond dealer who may have a call for a sapphire. The first thing a colored stone dealer will do when shown a colored gem is to put it on his fingers and look down without the use of an eye loupe in order to examine the stone for color. The first thing a diamond dealer does when shown a stone is to grip it fiercely with a pair of tweezers and immediately apply a jeweler's loupe to it. Color in a diamond can be seen very clearly by a trained jeweler's eye through a loupe, especially when the stone is viewed through the girdle, or edge, of a stone. In any case, white is white, and the major nightmare for a diamond dealer is not that the color may be off, but rather that there may be some incredible flaw within a stone—and that is what he is looking for.

Put a Ceylon sapphire on a table before an Antwerp diamond merchant and invariably, within one second, he will inspect it through a loupe. The facets of a Ceylon sapphire appear so helter-skelter and misproportioned that from the diamond dealer's viewpoint the cutter might as well have been drunk while he cut the stone! Nothing could be further from the truth. Ceylon sapphire cutters have a most difficult problem: the color often radiates from one portion of the stone; other portions of the stone may be pale or even colorless. The cutter's art is to angle the piece of rough in such a way as to bring this spot of color closest to the table of the stone. Symmetry is invariably sacrificed to achieve depth of color.

In addition to newly mined sapphires from Thailand and Ceylon, large numbers of very fine stones are appearing throughout the world via secondhand jewelry pieces. At auctions and through estate settlements, a New York gem dealer can buy quality stones that often may be superior to stones found at any given time in the Far East.

Melee

When shopping for loose gems, you can see thousands of carats of small, round stones approximately the size of a small letter on this page (2 to 3 mm. in diameter). These stones are called "melee," the French word for confusion. They are sold in large boxes by the thousands, and their colors vary markedly. Ring manufacturers worldwide buy these stones to set with diamonds in cocktail rings and other jewelry. A typical cocktail ring might contain five sapphire stones worth $3 each and five diamonds worth $20 each, as well as a gold mounting. The whole ring would sell for $200 to $300 in a local retail store.

Sapphire melee, along with ruby melee, emerald melee, and diamond melee, account for the vast percentage of precious stones in the world: far greater in weight than the single carat size stones. The reason lies in the method of formation of the precious stone rough.

Generally speaking, a piece of rough is so flawed internally that only a tiny portion of it—perhaps 1 percent—can be used to facet a gemstone. Just a little squiggle at the end of the rough is clear and consistent in color. This tiny piece will become material for a faceted round stone.

How to Value a Sapphire

In the last three years, sapphire prices have increased by a factor of two, if not by more, and a quality gemstone on a wholesale basis sells at a price often exceeding $5,000 per carat. This is for the finest quality stone of a Burmese or Kashmir color that is fairly well proportioned. As mentioned earlier, the best way to ascertain value is to have a comparative selection of sapphires in different shades of blue and different levels of clarity and proportion. Shade of color is the most important price factor.

V

How to Invest in Emeralds

History of Emeralds

Like rubies and sapphires, emeralds have a long and interesting history, which I shall touch upon only briefly.

In ancient Egypt, emeralds were mined not far from the Nile. Judging by the quality of Egyptian emerald jewelry, we know that their stones were of a spotty, light color variety. This tranquil green color was much prized in the Egyptian world, although it is not very popular among dealers and investors today, as finer grades of emeralds have been discovered.

Emeralds in ancient Rome were valued for the cool, calming effect of their color. Nero watched the Roman games in the Coliseum; when he tired, he would peer at the exhibition through emerald glasses.

It was not until much later, however—at the time of the Spanish capture of Central and South America in the sixteenth century—that fine emeralds really entered the gem world of Europe.

The first precious stones found in a mine tend to be the largest and most beautiful. The deeper one goes into the earth, the less perfect the color and the less pure the crystallization. When Pizarro and Cortez subdued the Americas, they claimed the great emerald and gold wealth of the Inca and Mayan civilizations for their native Spain. As these stones were the first fruits of the rich mines of the Americas, it is believed that the finest examples of emeralds came from this period in history.

Many of the first fine South American emeralds were shipped to India through the trading ports of the Philippines. Some Chinese still call emerald the "Filipino stone." A study of the inclusion patterns of the emeralds in the collection of the Moghul rulers of Delhi reveal that these gems originated in the mines of Colombia.

In Pizarro's time, the mines at Muzo and Chivor had been working, but they were covered up and hidden by the Indians before the Spaniards could seize them. The mineral wealth of the Mayan civilization was more than a sign of affluence. The Mayans believed that their gold, silver, and emeralds were direct gifts from the gods, and the gems held a prominent place in all celebrations. Given the religious significance of these precious gems, it is no wonder that the Mayan and Incan people, even under torture, refused to disclose the whereabouts of their emerald mines. A jungle enclosed these Colombian mines in much the same way that the Angkor Wat temple lay covered by the jungle in Cambodia, until it was discovered after a thousand years by a wandering Parisian tourist. In 1895, traces of emeralds were found near Muzo, and that ancient and fabulous mine was reopened. Chivor was rediscovered in the 1920s.

There are other sources of emeralds besides Egypt and Colombia. Emeralds have been found in Russia—unmistakably pale in color—and in small quantities in Austria and India. More recently, emeralds have been discovered in Brazil, Rhodesia, Zambia, and Afghanistan.

Mining Emeralds

Emeralds are not found along riverbanks like diamonds, rubies, and sapphires, but are imbedded in the rock itself; this accounting for the high price of extraction. Emerald deposits are often found in conjunction with layers of mica schist. They also often run along pegmatite dikes. A small pocket of emeralds might well be located by cutting through the mica area. This is extremely laborious work.

The recently discovered mines near Carnaiba, Brazil, provide an example of what an emerald strike is like. About fifteen years ago, the Brazilian government decided to build its section of the Pan American highway, linking numerous countries in North and South America with Central America. This huge and ambitious road project meant, in effect, that people with a high degree of geological engineering skills were sent from the capital and from Rio to the very underdeveloped hinterlands. As these roadbuilders cut roads through the jungles of Brazil, they uncovered incredible sources of mineral wealth.

Rumors circulated that there were pockets of emeralds near Carnaiba. Within weeks, vast numbers of Brazilians descended upon this small town to begin mining on the most primitive scale. Tens of thousands of claims were filed with the government. The Brazilian government has long favored the protection of the small miner; at one time there were twenty thousand mines with separate shafts going into the ground in Carnaiba.

In the center of town, where traffic is most dense and a rotary has been built, there exists an emerald mine of about fifty feet across and two hundred feet straight down. Similarly, in the back of stores, in front of people's homes, there are small-scale mines being dug and worked each day. Workers are lowered into the mines on ropes, where they gouge out rocks with the simplest of hand tools. Blasting is an impossibility because it might destroy the fragile emerald crystals. Once they are pried from the bottom of the mine, the rocks are hoisted up with a pulley system to be sorted and evaluated by a partner aboveground. Generally, the mines are a cooperative effort on the part of three or four individuals. The output of the mines is traded either in Carnaiba itself or in Rio de Janeiro.

Carnaiba gives the appearance of being a "gold rush" boom town, with its tens of thousands of wandering and hopeful prospectors, its dance halls, bordellos, and its strange, transient beauty. One has a feeling that if the mines were to run out, the town would become a jungle within several weeks and its entire population would travel to another part of Brazil with the same idea of striking it rich through a combination of luck and hard work.

Judging the Color of Emeralds

The emerald reveals much of its origin through the shade of green visible to the eye. I remember a 2 carat Muzo Colombian emerald of a very rich green color which was in our office. Upon seeing it, an elderly French colored stone dealer said: "This is what we used to call a wild color —*une couleur sauvage.*" He explained that in Paris in the 1920s and 1930s, this particular shade of green was immediately recognized not only as coming from Colombia but as originating in Muzo.

Similarly, a more bluish green has been identified as coming from the mines of Chivor. Colombian stones in general possess a deep color that is preferred by most collectors —in comparison to the Russian emeralds of the nineteenth century that tended towards a patchy, very pale green.

The Sandawana emeralds from Rhodesia are a very deep, rich green color; but the size of the crystals has been so small that they are most appropriate for small, round, or melee stones.

Brazilian emeralds are characterized by an even lighter shade of color than the Russian emeralds, although new mines have been discovered recently in which the quality appears to be more promising. Emeralds were mined in India centuries ago. They had a deep bluish cast to the green and today are highly prized by dealers and investors in fine gems.

What gives an emerald this green tint? The chromium within the emerald crystal is composed of aluminum oxide and accounts for the depth of color. If a stone has 1/100th of 1 percent too much chromium, what will remain is a very blackish bluish green emerald. Similarly, a 1/100th of 1 percent difference in the chromium count might result in an extremely yellowish green stone. Grading emeralds is said to be among the most difficult tasks in precious stone dealings, and it is a terriffic help to have other fine emeralds on hand against which to evaluate the stone in question.

A large number of emeralds fall into the melee category. These stones, varying between 2, 3, and 4 millimeters in size, constitute the bulk of dollar volume of emeralds traded in the world today. Most emerald crystals are opaque, with very little usable material within a crystal. Therefore, a small, thin sliver of clear green at the edge of a piece of rough can be utilized to make a tiny round stone; that is what happens in a great number of cases.

One can see Indian colored stone merchants traveling throughout the world to every mining center of Brazil, Africa, and elsewhere. These dealers will buy tens of thousands of carats and ship them back to India, where they will be cut and faceted by thousands of Indian gem cutters. Gem cutting in India has existed for over two thousand years. On a roof in Bombay, for example, there may be a group of ten cutters who will use the most rudimentary of tools—a wheel that is turned by hand and a cutting device so primitive that it has not changed in several hundred years. And day after day, year after year, century after century, these Hindus, Moslems, and Jains have fashioned under that incredibly bright Indian sky the majority of the world's emeralds. The destination of these emeralds can be a ring that is interspersed with emeralds and diamonds, or simply a complicated pin or necklace using the small round emeralds.

Rough buyers purchase all grades and sizes of crystals. Generally speaking, emerald rough is sold in 50,000-piece, 100,000-piece, and even larger lots. Every rough dealer of emeralds throughout the world who is worth his salt has put aside a few fine emerald rough pieces as a kind of saving for the future. And there are, of course, legends about these dealers. One man supposedly has a houseful. Another, in Brazil, has a treasure chest containing rough that will yield over five carats for each stone. But these are legends. The fact is that fine emeralds are becoming more scarce each day. In my observation, the vast majority of fine emeralds on the

How to Invest in Emeralds

market have actually been set in pieces of jewelry for the last fifty years. Only now are they beginning to be taken from mountings and recut to give them better color and brilliance. Very exciting emeralds have been bought in our office as part of old estate pieces of jewelry.

How to Distinguish Genuine from Synthetic Emeralds

Synthetic emeralds are made by mixing aluminum oxide with traces of chromium under high heat and large amounts of pressure. There are two great makers of synthetic emeralds in the world today, and they are extremely secretive about their methods of operation.

Caryl Chatham and his son from San Francisco, California, have developed a most remarkable, exceedingly beautiful emerald. Chatham has priced his product in the hundreds of dollars per carat, and he refuses to discuss his production methods. Similarly, in the south of France, another technological genius, Pierre Gilson, has utilized a method of creating synthetic emeralds.

The secret in distinguishing the natural from the man-made emerald may lie in the inclusions. A natural emerald is created over the course of millions of years, and the inclusions are a shorthand diary of that stone's birth pains and growth history. The short, perhaps month-long, history of the creation of the synthetic emerald has another set of inclusions that betray that gemstone's man-made origins.

Under the microscope, one can see wispy, veillike inclusions permeating the Chatham or Gilson emeralds. These contrast with the included crystals of pyrite, calcite, and actinolite that dot the interior landscape of a naturally formed emerald crystal.

Similarly, man-made emeralds become easily activated under ultraviolet light, appearing reddish, while natural emeralds do not appear to light up. This test is not hard to perform. One word of caution, however: after a few years' study, the ingenious Mr. Gilson managed to mix an amount of iron with his synthetic emeralds; this prevented any fluorescence. Nonetheless, the Gemological Institute of America has been able to analyze the chemical compositions and impurities in this emerald by means of a spectroscope.

How to Value an Emerald

There are no industrial uses for emeralds as there are for diamonds. Consequently, an emerald mine owner's only profit is from the sale of his gemstones. If there is no gem content in his mine, the mine simply cannot be worked. As diamond melee has gone up to $200 to $300 per carat for finer stones, so too, emerald melee has sharply increased in price over the past few years. It is not unusual on a wholesale level to see emeralds selling for $700 to $800 per carat of melee, which often translates into $70 to $80 per stone—a stone the size of the letter "o" on this page.

The stones, however, that capture the dealer's and investor's imagination are mainly the bigger stones—those that are cut into carat sizes or better. Emeralds over 10 carats are a great, great rarity. However, unlike rubies, which had to be presented to the king if they exceeded 6 carats, emeralds were never placed under this constraint in Colombia or in other gem-mining areas. Consequently, we can see in the Smithsonian Institution two emeralds that are over 30 carats, of superb, sealike transparency.

The popularity of emeralds has been so strong in recent years that most auctions offer at least one important stone for sale. Even if you have no immediate intention of buying an emerald, an auction is a good place in which to become familiar with its various shades of color and market value.

If you want to get an idea of the full, delicate range of the emerald colors, there is no question but that a trip to the Iranian collection of precious stones would easily be the finest education possible. Barring this, the same mechanics are involved in purchasing an emerald as in purchasing other precious gems. Ultimately, you will depend upon the reputation, knowledge, and skill of the establishment or person from whom you are buying the gem. It is thus wise to find,

How to Invest in Emeralds

by means of inquiry, who in your town has an understanding ear and a stock of emeralds for sale. *And* arm yourself in advance with as much knowledge of the subject as possible.

One thing that always shocks a new investor is the fact that almost every emerald contains some blemishes or inclusions. Although it seems incredible that one could pay several thousands of dollars for a stone that is not perfectly flawless, the overwhelming factor in the price of emeralds is the strength and purity of its green color. Flawless emeralds are nonexistent!

Finally, by comparing the sizes of the stones, the shades of green, and the relative absence of flaws with the price of a stone, one can normally make a decision as to which emerald is most suitable for purchase.

VI

Comparative Prices of Rubies, Sapphires, and Emeralds in the Past Seven Years

It is rather difficult to state exactly what the price for a superb ruby, sapphire, or emerald should be, as each stone has an individual "personality" and is slightly different from other stones. However, the price increase in the past years has been considerable. A stone should be held for a long period of time—at least five years—and the fact that prices have gone up in the past does not necessarily mean they will go up in the future.

Rubies

In May 1969, in Geneva, a 3.25 carat "specimen ruby was auctioned for $4,600 per carat. A similar group of 3 specimen rubies, of 4 carat size, was sold at the Geraldine Rockefeller Dodge sale at Parke-Bernet Galleries for $18,000 per carat.

Sapphires

In May 1970, in Geneva, Christie's auctioned a superb 48 carat sapphire for $1,300 a carat. A similar quality stone, a

This crown is in the collection of gems in the Bank Melli, Teheran, Iran. It is worn by the wife of the Shah of Iran on state occasions. The emeralds are of top color, perfectly matched, but not flawless. Internally flawless emeralds are virtually unknown. Emeralds are valued primarily on color.

Photograph courtesy of the Bank Melli, Iran

These commercial quality emeralds are average color and clarity. Each emerald would sell for $2,000 to $3,000 apiece.

Photograph by John Cubito

Fine color emerald. The tiny diamonds and the gold mounting account for little of the resale value; however a well-mounted emerald can be worn and enjoyed; in addition, it can be auctioned. Thus the mounting's beauty is, in fact, most important.

Photograph by Reid Rutherford

Emerald crystallizes in a six-sided (hexagonal) pattern in the earth. Because of its fragility, no blasting is done in emerald mining and the recovery costs are high.

Photograph courtesy of the American Museum of Natural History

Above Ruby often crystallizes in calcite. Traces of ruby are exceedingly rare with almost no new mines having been discovered in the last one thousand years.

*Photograph courtesy of the
American Museum of Natural History*

Below The author, examining sapphire rough in Sri Lanka (Ceylon). Stones have been found in the Ceylon rivers as well as in the ground for the past two thousand years and have been sold to traveling gem merchants since the days of Marco Polo.

Photograph by Fred Malvena

The author, examining and comparing sapphires in the Precious Stones Company office in New York City. In order to ascertain value, sapphires and all colored stones should be compared one to another. In the background is a picture of Charles Zucker and Kantzwai.

Photograph by Peter Schaaf

Above Ceylon (Sri Lanka) miner. The miners in Ceylon have often mined the same land for centuries. *Below* Ceylon miner holding a wicker basket in the water. The sapphire and ruby sink to the bottom of the basket. The other lighter stones float away. This "panning" method is also used in gold and diamond separations.

Photographs by Fred Malvena

Above Cut orange grossularite garnet, incorrectly called "semi-precious." Gems other than ruby, sapphire, emerald, and diamond have appreciated strongly over the past five years.
Below left Cut tourmaline at $200 per carat.
Below right Crystal specimen that is dramatic.

Photograph by Reid Rutherford

Comparative Prices 41

superb 28 carat sapphire, was auctioned in May 1975 for $6,100 per carat. Just recently, at the remarkable Geraldine Rockefeller Dodge sale in New York at Parke-Bernet Galleries on October 15, 1975, a 40 carat "magnificent" sapphire was auctioned for $7,500 per carat.

Emeralds

At the Enid Haupt sale in 1972, there was a 34 carat beautiful emerald sold for $10,000 a carat. Such a stone, if it were to come on the market today, would easily sell for twice that price, which is more than three times its price in 1968, when it sold for $6,000 per carat.

For medium grade rubies, sapphires, and emeralds, price increases have also been exceptionally dramatic.

VII

How to Invest in Diamonds

The Origins of Diamonds

The original source of the diamond is the very depths of the earth. Under the stable, relatively unchanging outer layer of earth is a sea of churning liquid—a molten substance, fiery and hot beyond imagination. This molten interior, or "magma," erupts from time to time through the earth's surface in a volcanic process. The remnants of such eruption and subsequent cooling in very rare cases create a long, thin shaft of a mineral called kimberlite, and kimberlite, in turn, contains diamond crystals in minute traces. Sometimes kimberlite and diamond crystal are weathered on the earth's surface; the crystal may come into contact with rivers and be carried away. In ancient India, such rare river-carried alluvial stones—diamonds—were cut in very rudimentary fashion and worn as talismans and magical symbols.

As early as the time of Alexander the Great, in the fourth century B.C., diamond mines were believed to exist in India. Legend has it that these mines were guarded by snakes and terrible demons. No one could approach the diamonds. But the wily Greeks supposedly figured out a ruse whereby they would slaughter sheep and throw the bits of meat into the diamond pit. The meat would adhere to the diamonds. Then vultures would retrieve the meat and diamond combination and discard the diamonds, which would be gathered by the

Greeks. Most myths and legends contain elements of historical truth; interestingly, diamonds do adhere to grease. Thus, such a story is not altogether impossible.

Diamonds played second fiddle to colored stones in the Middle Ages, and it was only in the early part of the fifteenth century that they gained popularity. Part of the credit for this increase in popularity must be given to Louis de Berquem, a Jewish diamond cutter from Bruges, Belgium, who developed a more sophisticated system of faceting to accentuate the brilliance of the stone.

Diamonds possess two optical characteristics that are somewhat in conflict, and cutters must take both into consideration when working on a stone. One is the stone's brilliance, defined as "the return of white light to the observer's eye." The other is its light which splits into many colors. This is called "dispersion."

In the 1600s, 1700s, and 1800s, what was sought in diamonds was this quality of dispersion. Diamonds were considered to be most beautiful when they shimmered in multicolored light. Consequently, stones were cut to accentuate this feature, and the top of the diamond, or table facet, was kept small—to enlarge it would cause less dispersion. In the late nineteenth century, however, there was a desire for balance between dispersion and brilliance, and the table thus became larger and slightly flatter in proportion to the stone.

For centuries, diamond cutting was a skill passed on within families and was very much of an experimental operation. When the Venetian diamond cutter Peruzzi was able to perfect a fifty-eight-facet stone in the early 1700s, diamonds truly came into their own.

The discovery of diamonds in Brazil in 1724 sent tremendous commercial shock waves throughout the world. Until that time, the same Indian diamond mines on the riverbanks had been worked for centuries. Indian diamond mines around Golconda employed over seventy thousand workers and were so intensively worked that by the early 1700s, most of the diamonds had been retrieved and production had begun to fall sharply.

The decline in production coincided with the increasing interest in diamonds to balance out the reds, blues, and greens of colored stones. Discovery of the Brazilian mines was therefore both fortuitous and timely.

When the huge Brazilian diamond mines were opened in 1724, diamonds were selling at all-time high prices because the supply from India had by then been exhausted. Gem merchants as well as bankers throughout the word reacted in predictable ways. First they denied that diamonds had been found in Brazil. Then they claimed that Brazilian diamonds were so hard that they could never be faceted, and were thus for the interest of collectors alone and would not have universal appeal.

The Brazilian diamond traders, a resourceful group who had to go deep into the interior of Brazil to retrieve the early diamonds, hit upon a rather clever scheme. Diamonds were transshipped from Brazil to Goa, where they were sold to London dealers as Indian-mined merchandise. After several years it became apparent that, in fact, the stones came from Brazil, and they were no more difficult to cut than Indian ones. This discovery suddenly flooded the market with diamonds, and the price fell very substantially.

Prices of Diamonds

In the late 1700s, Jeffreys formulated his rule of squares (similar to Tavernier's rule of squares), which stated that knowing the base price for a precious stone (diamond) of 1 carat would enable one to ascertain the value of a 3 or 4 carat stone. In other words, if a 1 carat diamond cost $2,000 per carat, a 2 carat diamond would cost $2,000 times two times two, which would be $8,000 for the stone. Similarly, a 3 carat diamond would cost $2,000 per carat (base price) times three times three—or a total of $18,000.

The base price or the price of a 1 carat stone is extremely important as it is the cornerstone on which all other prices are computed. In the above example, the per carat price of a 1 carat stone is $2,000, the per carat price of a 2 carat stone is $4,000, and the per carat price of a 3 carat stone is $6,000 per carat. This geometric progression is related to the fact that large stones are much rarer than small stones.

Prices of Colored Stones and Diamonds

The table in Appendix 1 contains the current prices of fine quality rubies, sapphires, emeralds, and diamonds. By gem quality I mean fine color, good clarity, and good cut.

The diamond prices are for D color flawless stones (according to the Gemological Institute of America's system of grading). The commercial diamonds are of a medium color (J color) and medium clarity (VVS). The prices are my own estimate and do not constitute an offer to buy or sell.

In the trade, the term "strawberries" refers to items on a price list that a dealer does not have and probably never had. Thus, when the retail store or customer calls and says he wants the pear-shaped diamond for $18,000 on page three of the price list, the dealer says, "I'm sorry, I'm fresh out of these; however, how about item 18?" That is a strawberry.

Remember that these are wholesale prices. The rule of thumb is that a retailer in any country, and particularly in the United States, must add a minimum of 30 percent onto the wholesale cost to arrive at the retail cost in order to conduct his business. Generally speaking, any individual should be willing to pay this retail markup unless he or she is prepared to buy in prohibitively large "wholesale lots." It may help to note that you are buying the "honesty" and "expertise" that are characteristic of the fine American retail jeweler. Because of the markup, however, gems must be considered long-term and not short-term investments.

VIII

The De Beers Diamond Syndicate and How It Stabilizes Prices

The Diamond Syndicate—Its History

Another reason for the sharp decrease in diamond prices in the late 1700s was the political upheaval in France—fleeing noblemen were forced to dispose of their gems quickly, flooding the market with diamonds. Both the Brazilian and French upheavals did not last more than five years, however, after which diamonds resumed their upward price spiral.

Meanwhile, in South Africa in the 1800s a historic event occurred. A small child noticed a shiny pebble and gave it to a wandering Irish trader named O'Reilly (a lucky name, according to Gaelic and American tradition). O'Reilly showed the stone to a South African geologist who identified it as a 21.25 carat diamond!

Like the Indian diamonds, the first South African diamonds were of river origin. Small concentrations of diamonds were discovered around the Orange River and soon a full-fledged diamond rush was under way. De Beers, a sober Boer farmer, found diamond crystals on his land and subsequently sold his property to miners at a very high price. Diamond fever spread through South Africa. Large numbers of prospectors came to the area from all over the world.

The De Beers Diamond Syndicate

The same "panning" method used to locate sapphire crystals was used for diamonds. Outcroppings of yellowish and bluish green mineral deposits were found near the town of Kimberly and came to be called kimberlite. The Kimberly mine turned out to be the richest diamond mine to be discovered in thousands of years, and has retained this distinction ever since.

The competition for diamonds resembled the gold rush of another day. Every few feet another miner had staked out a claim and began digging into the ground. Gradually, the earth around Kimberly was dug in such a helter-skelter fashion, with so many interconnecting tunnels, that large-scale cave-ins began to occur.

A Few Personalities

Two of the main characters who emerged at that time were Cecil Rhodes, known to the world as the creator of the De Beers diamond syndicate, and Barney Barnato, a fabulous though less well known personality. Barnato came to South Africa with his brother from the Jewish East End district of London in the hopes of making his fortune as a song-and-dance man, a comedian, a boxer, basically as an all-around entertainer. After some years, he started to trade in various products, including ostrich feathers (South Africa, as my father, Charles Zucker, can tell you, has some of the loveliest ostrich feathers in the world), sugar, and spices. But as everyone knew in the 1880s, the true wealth of South Africa lay in its newly discovered diamond areas.

With the money he made as a trader, Barnato began to accumulate large holdings in different sections of the Kimberly mine. Eventually, he formed his own very profitable mining and trading company.

Cecil Rhodes, an Oxford-trained classicist and a year older than Barnato, was of quite a different disposition and character. Where Barnato was gregarious, easygoing, and shrewd, Rhodes was taciturn and careful. Rhodes came to South Africa as an adventurer eager to create an empire, and he soon became involved in mining at the Kimberly diamond fields. It did not take him long to see the necessity of uniting the diamond miners into a cooperative cartel, of eliminating the reigning chaos, increasing production, and creating safer working conditions.

Rhodes suggested to Barnato that they consolidate and form one large company under the De Beers Corporation banner, which could market all the Kimberly diamonds. Barnato also foresaw the need for centralization of diamond selling. However, he felt that Rhodes should sell out to him and that he, as the better trader, should be the dominant figure in the Kimberly area.

But Rhodes was determined to remain in command. Since he did not have the capital to fight Barnato, he cleverly went back to Europe and, with the aid of a consortium headed by the Rothschilds, kept the pressure on Barnato as they both tried to buy up remaining claims in the Kimberly area.

Finally, after several years of conflict, the two men came to an agreement. Barnato became the president and Rhodes the chairman of the newly formed De Beers Consolidated Mining Company, Ltd. They then proceeded to buy up other diamond areas and establish a very strong position in the gold-mining areas of South Africa.

In 1899, the De Beers syndicate controlled at least 90 percent of the world's production of diamonds. In the next ten years new mines were discovered in South Africa; the De Beers Corporation, despite its somewhat meager cash position, was able to buy up these units of production.

Barnato's life did not end happily. He moved from success to success, becoming the largest builder and owner of property within the city of Johannesburg, developing countless gold-mining areas as well as factory sites throughout South Africa. Yet he suffered increasingly from bouts of melancholy; at the age of forty-six, on a voyage back from London, he committed suicide. His firm continued its operation, controlled by his brother, nephews, and assorted cousins, and has remained a dominant factor in diamonds, gold, and real estate.

Rhodes, a highly nervous man, also died at an early age

The Oppenheimer family in South Africa. Photo by N.W. Ayres.

after suffering disgrace in South Africa's political scene. The vision of these two men, however, set the stage for one of the most remarkable of modern business structures—the De Beers diamond syndicate.

In the early 1900s, another figure who would figure prominently in the De Beers history, Sir Ernest Oppenheimer, came to South Africa as a broker for a London diamond firm. He achieved a position of importance by acquiring diamond mine holdings in Southwest Africa. However, when the crash of 1929 hit the De Beers syndicate in full force and diamond prices fell to 50 percent of their predepression peak (each day fetching new, lower quotations), Sir Ernest proposed that the diamond syndicate draw even closer together. He affiliated his own company and the Anglo–American Corporation in a complex fashion, along with the De Beers company. Sir Ernest became the head of the De Beers Consolidated Mining Company, Ltd. During the ensuing depression, De Beers was able to sharply curtail production in most mines, going so far as to completely stop production in four of the five large diamond pipe areas. This far-sighted and dramatic move stabilized the price of diamonds, which fell only marginally after 1932 and began a climb after World War II that has reached extraordinary heights.

As the head of De Beers, Sir Ernest Oppenheimer emphasized the value of conservatism, a policy continued by his son, Harry Oppenheimer. In the period of prosperity following World War II, De Beers consistently attempted to build an extremely strong foundation for all its interlocking mining and financial interests—"hoping for the best and expecting the worst."

The Diamond Trading Company has, over the years, built up a network of two hundred and fifty dealers who travel to London ten times a year to receive "sights" from the syndicate.

What kind of people are these dealers? A brief look at the personality of a successful diamond trader will give you some idea. Diamond dealers are generally reluctant to speak about the history of their business, but it has been my good

Harry Oppenheimer negotiating a contract for the production of diamonds. Photo by N.W. Ayres.

Gutman Gutwirth studying the Talmud. The author's grandfather was both a leading diamond merchant and a rabbi in Antwerp before World War II.

fortune to be the son of a rabbi's daughter whose father was, at the same time, a diamond dealer.

My grandfather, Gutman Gutwirth (HaCohen), grew up in a very poor family in Cracow, Poland, the extremely beautiful and historic capital city. When my grandfather was in his teens, he went to study in a famous Talmudist's house; he was considered to be a great Talmudic genius even at a young age.

The rabbi with whom my grandfather lived and studied had a daughter a year younger than Gutman Gutwirth. The two children were betrothed at the age of seventeen. My grandfather went to his Hasidic rabbi, the Belzer Rabbi, and told him that "he wanted to go to western Europe because he found making a living in Cracow very difficult." One question nagged my grandfather: If he and his wife were to travel to a more cosmopolitan society, would he, like so many Jews before him, become less religious? After thinking for a short time, the old Belzer Rabbi said, "Gutman Gutwirth, wherever you go, and whatever you do, you will always be a religious Jew."

My grandfather went to Antwerp, where he became a diamond broker and cutter. After work, he would stay up until 2 or 3 A.M. studying the Talmud. There is a saying that the Talmud is like the ocean—from whichever angle it is looked at, it seems to change. So it must have been for my grandfather, who, for the rest of his life, continued to study in a small group of religious Jews in Antwerp.

He had a large family of four sons and five daughters, and after he began to prosper during the early part of the twentieth century, he lived on quite a lavish scale. His specialty was his ability to peer into a rough diamond and guess how large a faceted stone could be obtained from the rough material. This ability is considered the most important skill in the diamond business. A diamond dealer must first look at a piece of rough and determine: what its internal flaws are; if there are unsightly blemishes, cleavages, or carbon spots; whether they can be cut away, leaving a smaller but clearer, more perfect finished stone; or, as is generally the case, if one cuts away the parts that have faults, is the remaining stone so small that one has lost money in the transaction? The problem, therefore, is to obtain the largest, purest, most internally clean stone possible, given the limits of the piece of rough itself.

Diamond rough dealers have traditionally been both quick and painstakingly careful. It is necessary, generally, to buy quickly in the rough market. But once a piece of rough has been purchased, it is not unusual, if it is of large size (yielding, for example, a diamond of perhaps 8 carats or more), to spend many months looking at the same diamond rough, trying to find the best way to cut the stone. I have always felt that there was a connection between my grandfather's great love and patience in studying the Talmud at night

The De Beers Diamond Syndicate

and his extraordinary skill and patience in examining rough diamonds during the day.

All my grandfather's sons became diamond dealers and traveled to France, Indonesia, Singapore, and Australia to purchase precious stones.

My uncle Aaron Gutwirth set up diamond-trading companies in the wilder sections of Indonesia. He was a large exporter of rough stones as well as of other products. After World War II, another uncle, Bernard Gutwirth, began a large diamond-trading company in France and set and mounted diamonds into rings. A third uncle, Hendrick Gutwirth, specialized in diamond trading in Australia. Finally, my uncle Henri Gutwirth, unlike the rest of the family, remained a diamond dealer in Antwerp.

Henri Gutwirth was fascinated by diamond rough. After the war, he was instrumental in helping the De Beers Consolidated Mining Company obtain mining rights in Angola. As a reward, and also because the Diamond Trading Company had such confidence in him and his family, he was given a "sight." He became president of the Antwerp Diamond Club and one of the most respected members of the diamond community there.

All of my uncles shared a tremendous respect for the diamond as a source of value and importance. Even my uncle Aaron Gutwirth, who became a major business figure in the

Examining rough diamonds. The skill is in deciding how the largest, finest stone can be cut from a given piece of rough diamond. Often the diamond rough is examined for many months before the cutting plan is decided upon. Photo by N.W. Ayres.

state of Israel and in the Far East, continued to expand the diamond portion of his interests. He felt that diamonds somehow were magical, and that in every country and in all times people would buy them.

After I finished studying law at Harvard and began to work in the colored stone field, I came into contact with precious stone dealers. Only then did I begin to understand the psychology and motivations of this rather amazing group of people who are so fascinated by precious stones.

The diamond syndicate has tried to find people who will mirror its own personality: diamond dealers who, first of all, have complete confidence in the diamond itself; people who keep their personal expenses down, reinvest their profits within their own industry, work tirelessly, and encourage their own children to enter the diamond business.

A kind of conservative sensibility permeates the Diamond Trading Company, a feeling that one should not talk about

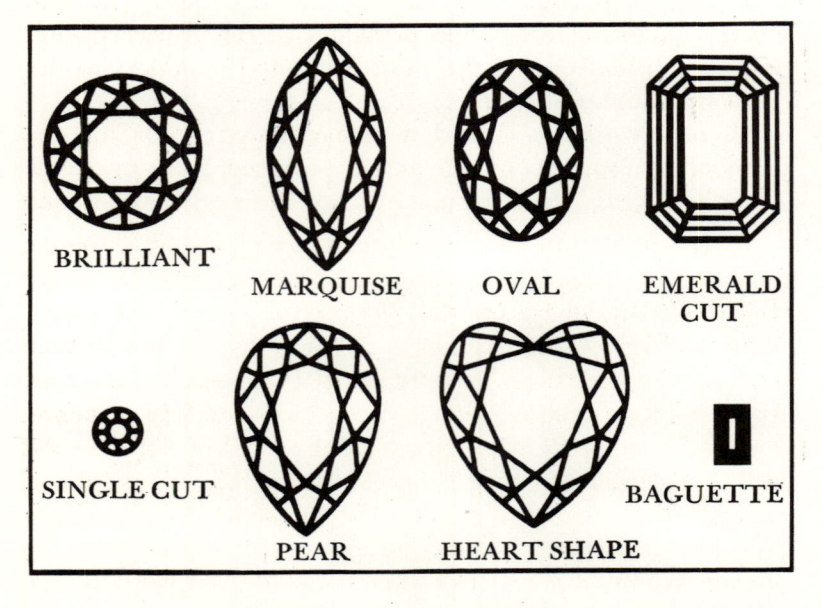

Shapes of stones. The round, brilliant-cut diamond is now the standard cut. However, all shapes are acceptable, provided the diamond is cut proportionately.

what one does except when necessary, and that one's actions should outweigh one's pronouncements.

Never, in the many years that De Beers has been a public company, has the corporation tried to hard-sell its stock. We all know that in the 1960s it was a common practice among American corporations to acquire other companies by issuing shares and then, each time earnings went up, to take out large advertisements in the major magazines and newspapers proclaiming how well their conglomerate activities were doing. In retrospect, it is easy to see how foolish these activities were. Here were publicly owned companies spending their shareholders' money in order to convince more people to buy their stock at inflated prices. Earnings were juggled from quarter to quarter in a false attempt to buoy stockholder interest. Rather than try to build a truly long-term, solid business foundation, the corporations were trying to impress their stockholders and the Wall Street analysts.

In 1974, for example, the De Beers Corporation had remarkable financial success. On sales of approximately $1.2 billion, the gross profit, after expenses and South African taxes, amounted to $350 million. This ratio is extraordinary, since for most mining companies the ratio is generally about 5 percent. Interestingly, the company paid approximately $150 million in dividends; at one point the shares were selling for about $3. Shares bought at that time were paying a 10 percent return, which is extremely high for the common stock of an established company. Nevertheless, De Beers shares, quoted daily in the *New York Times* and major financial publications, had fallen from a high of $10. In such a case, I am absolutely certain that if De Beers had been an American corporation with a keen public relations sense, it would have done two things: Harry Oppenheimer would have called a press conference in South Africa and stated that he was greatly increasing the dividend on his shares; and he would have said that since the shares were so abysmally low in price, the parent company would be buying shares on the open market in large quantities.

These two measures would undoubtedly have pushed up the price of De Beers shares to two or three times their then current value. But what would it all have meant? After all, De Beers is not interested in what the public thinks of its diamond business. It is more interested in keeping its mining costs down and its long-term diamond sales firm. In the past ten years, there has been no significant upward movement in the price of De Beers shares. They have alternately gone up and down, although earnings have risen dramatically and company reserves have increased markedly. And it must be remembered that this is what enabled De Beers to stabilize the diamond prices worldwide.

The Political Situation

Because of De Beers' extensive diamond-mining activities in South Africa, it stands to reason that the company would be concerned about black–white relations there. The fear that blacks may eventually confiscate or nationalize white-owned businesses is a real one; but it is to be hoped that if South Africa will upgrade the quality of life for all of its people, both white and black, chaos may be avoided.

In any case, De Beers is not the spokesman for South African political leaders. To the contrary, Harry Oppenheimer has formed his own political party, the Progressive Party. He is a long-time advocate of higher wages for the black worker and for liberalization of the national policies of South Africa. He has been a consistent thorn of conscience in the government's side.

The source of his strength in his struggle with the government has been the fact that 10 percent of the country's exports are directly attributable to the Anglo–American Corporation, to the De Beers company, and other Oppenheimer-headed enterprises.

There is no doubt that the De Beers company sees the racial situation in South Africa as an extremely complex, dangerous, and important problem that must be dealt with successfully if any long-term business commitments are to be sustained. What Harry Oppenheimer has done is to diversify out of diamonds into other endeavors.

These are the finest rubies in the world. The color matching is very exact. Many stones are larger than 10 carats, making this belt buckle valued in the millions of dollars. This is part of the Irani collection.

Photograph courtesy of Royal Ontario Museum.
Crown jewels of Iran. Photograph by Leighton Warren.

Emeralds in the Teheran Museum collection. The emeralds came from Colombia in the sixteenth century through the Spanish conquistadores. They are the top green and bluish green color.
*Photographs courtesy of Royal Ontario Museum.
Crown jewels of Iran. Photographs by Leighton Warren.*

A 170 carat emerald. This belt buckle contains a stone that is far larger than any emerald mined today. The recent emeralds are inferior in both size and quality to the "old mine" production.
Photograph courtesy of Royal Ontario Museum.
Crown jewels of Iran. Photograph by Leighton Warren.

This crown was designed by Pierre Arpels of Paris. The crown is more modern in feeling than others in the Teheran collection. The red stones are spinels, not rubies.

Photograph courtesy of Royal Ontario Museum.
Crown jewels of Iran. Photograph by Leighton Warren.

Trade beads. All primitive cultures, and most civilized ones, have beads that are worn commonly. Among beads, the highest valued is the eye, which is related to the gem and a mother's eyes—hence the psychological allure of gems.

Photograph courtesy of W. W. Norton, New York, from The Universal Bead *by Joan Erickson, 1969*

One can discern a circular bead pattern in Van Gogh's "Starry Night" painting. In Van Gogh's vision gems = beads = the stars in the heavens.

Photograph courtesy of Museum of Modern Art (Bequest of Lillie P. Bliss)

Detail of jewelry box of Renaissance woman.
Photograph courtesy of The Musée des Beaux Arts, Dijon, France

Detail of Indian necklace. Each emerald bead will be cut into two, and faceted into a gem emerald.
Photograph courtesy of McGraw-Hill, from Gregor Gregoretti's Jewelry through the Ages

This Jewish marriage ring is an example of enameling in Renaissance Italy. Enameling often replaced the need for rubies, sapphires, emeralds, and diamonds. Gradually, precious stones replaced enameling, until today the typical ring is almost all "center stone" and, unfortunately, little craftsmanship.

Photograph from the author's collection by Peter Schaaf

How Diamonds Are Priced and How Prices Are Stabilized

The stated policy of the diamond syndicate in its last few annual reports has been to distribute enough diamonds to satisfy world demand. However, even more important than this has been the diamond syndicate's attempt to maintain the diamond prices slightly ahead of the inflation rate of the American dollar.

If the inflation rate goes up 10 percent during a particular year, the diamond syndicate raises its price, say, 10.5 percent. Rough dealers receive consignments of rough, then pass along this price increase to cutters, and ultimately the increases are passed on to the retail customer. However, if a perfect D color, internally flawless stone of 1 carat which sold for $6,000 the previous year is offered at $6,650, no one can force the consumer to buy that stone, and he may refuse. If there is resistance to diamond prices at the higher level, the diamond syndicate simply cuts down on the number of diamonds offered at the next sight.

In other words, the purchaser of diamonds, even if he balks initially at higher prices, has never encountered great problems in selling his diamonds because the supply is regulated by the diamond syndicate. De Beers has even gone so far, it is said, as to purchase cut stones in the open market rather than allow any dramatic decline in price.

All this is fine so long as De Beers has the economic power to continue to buy the overhanging supply if the public is not interested and to withhold new supplies from the market.

The assets of the De Beers syndicate now far exceed $1 billion, and the entire Anglo–American group has perhaps $2 to $3 billion of additional assets that can readily be turned into liquid assets, if necessary, to support the long-term inventorying of diamonds.

I think, however, that if business were seriously depressed over a period of perhaps five years, De Beers might have difficulty maintaining a price schedule at high levels. Yet it has been shown repeatedly that when diamond demand falls in one area of the world, it tends to rise in another area. Even in the Great Depression of the thirties, there were parts of the world, particularly Europe, that were quite prosperous, and the demand for diamonds was fairly brisk. Diamond and colored stone prices fell far less than the United States stock market did during the Depression.

What is to keep a giant American corporation like General Motors or Du Pont from examining the De Beers balance sheet and deciding to go into the diamond-prospecting business in, say, the Congo, Sierra Leone, Angola, or Ghana? In my opinion, their reluctance to do so lies in their lack of background and expertise. Consider the following story:

In 1953, an African school child in Botswana found an tiny, low-quality diamond crystal at the edge of a cattle-feeding area. Two other cleavages were found, indicating the possible presence of diamond material. De Beers sent its geologists for a closer examination of the Botswana area.

Botswana is a large, landlocked country eking out an extremely poor living by cattle raising. A portion of Botswana is in the Kalahari desert. The geologists proceeded to draw up extensive geological surveys of the entire country. However, after two years of probing, no single diamond crystal was found. But De Beers is truly persistent in searching for diamonds. Rather than drop the project, as most corporations would have done, the company drew up an amazing plan.

The De Beers interest in finding diamonds is always twofold: First, they want the diamonds, and second, they do not want anyone else to get the diamonds because the other party might market the gems in the wrong way at the wrong time, thereby cheapening De Beers' extensive diamond inventory, as well as reducing the public's confidence in the inevitability of long-term price increases in the stone. So the De Beers plan was simply this:

An on-the-spot team of highly trained geologists recruited hundreds of Botswana citizens who collected a sample rock every ten yards. The samples were transported to the South African laboratories, where they were studied either for dia-

The De Beers Diamond Syndicate

mond or possibly garnet or olivine crystals—which often signal the presence of diamonds.

Looking at a wall map of Botswana, one can see the immense journey these geologists made; starting in the southeastern corner of the country, they marched northward over a period of years. No luck. Several years later, they began to walk ten yards by ten yards in a westerly direction. It took twelve years of searching, but finally, near Orapa, a watering station in western Botswana, a promising group of diamond crystals was found. The area was immediately core-drilled extensively, and an enormous "pipe" of diamonds has been found. Certainly, no American corporation would have spent the time and the money for such a long-term project.

Processing Diamond Crystals

Kimberly and the other major diamond-mining areas are remnants of volcanic activities within the earth that seeped to the surface and solidified, forming a massive kimberlite deposit that contains crystals of diamonds. There are only

The big hole outside of Kimberly, South Africa. Thousands of tons of earth were removed and sifted for diamonds. Photo courtesy of N.W. Ayres.

seven major known pipes of consequence in South Africa. And even when such a so-called rich vein of diamonds is found, it is a major undertaking to extract diamonds from that deposit. Generally speaking, it takes about twenty tons of rock to produce 4.5 carats of diamonds.

It is incredible when one thinks that a 1 carat diamond ring represents truckload after truckload of rock that had to be sorted, crushed, graded, and processed. Because of the large rock tonnage, De Beers has perfected many labor-saving devices to process kimberlite. The rock is retrieved by automatic drilling equipment and loaded onto huge open dump trucks. These trucks convey the rock to large crushing bins. The rocks are then fed through a system of grills and meshes where they are sorted into still smaller sizes.

Human eyes are watching these conveyor belts as they move along, and it is extremely rare for a large diamond crystal to be lost by accident. Such a loss of even one large crystal would negate a year's profits. Diamonds adhere to grease and not to water. This fact has enabled the diamond syndicate to perfect a grease table where diamonds stick to the moving conveyor and from which the other rock can be expelled, leaving the diamonds.

Finally, diamonds fluoresce. If an ultraviolet bulb is lit over the stones—and there is a technique that enables fluorescents to light up a diamond—a special mechanism can select that fluorescent diamond, automatically leaving the other nonfluorescent rocks moving along the conveyor belt.

Because of these extensive labor-saving devices, diamonds can be extracted and processed on a very economical basis. When the Orapa mines were tested intensively, De Beers concluded that the Orapa pipe was as promising as some of the large, previously discovered mines in the Kimberly area. Consequently, a huge complex was built employing the latest recovery devices. Workers from Botswana as well as from other areas of Africa were signed up on a six-month contract to work the mines. De Beers arranged a profit-sharing agreement with the government of Botswana, giving the government approximately 50 percent of the profits from the mines. The trick, of course, was to give away enough of the future profits to entice that government to agree to the arrangement and to honor the agreement, while at the same time keeping enough for De Beers to make the mining economically profitable.

Wages for the black Africans who work the mines have always been shockingly low. However, De Beers miners receive higher wages than their brothers, the poor cattle herders in Botswana. As a result, the Botswana government has been extremely anxious to develop the mining industry. De Beers has found that it is extremely important to set up a self-enclosed work compound for the black workers. The company deposits most of the workers' salaries in a bank that holds it for them until completion of their six-month contract.

Salaries have increased approximately 25 percent per year for the past several years. Typically, a worker will take the money and return to his native village, where he will buy a few head of cattle or set himself up in a much-improved position. Another benefit for local governments is the tendency for the development of diamond-mining areas to create an infrastructure of roads, communications networks, and human skills that in turn will spark an economic boom throughout Africa.

The Botswana mines have been so successful that they now account for approximately 25 percent of the entire De Beers production of diamonds (2.5 million carats per year).

One reason for De Beers' success is its willingness to send geologists to any part of the world to explore the possibility of the presence of diamonds. The parent company is unceasing in its efforts to find and develop diamond-mining areas. At the same time, the top people at De Beers are extremely honest, shrewd, and tough in their bargaining methods with diamond-mining countries. This skill cannot be overestimated. Recent developments in the Middle East show that it is not enough for companies to have industrial knowledge and the technical ability to extract minerals from unyielding geological formations. If these skills are not accompanied by political sensitivity, there is an overwhelming chance that nationalization will follow in time. Again, if these large, multinational corporations are to succeed, they must know how to give away enough and yet retain profits. Any lack of balance will result either in nationalization or bankruptcy.

Russian Diamonds: Who Will Win—the De Beers Diamond Syndicate or the Soviet Union?

De Beers faces a major crisis today as a result of the new discoveries of diamonds in the Soviet Union. Unfortunately, very little first-class research has been done by De Beers on inclusion patterns in diamonds. There is no monograph, for example, on the differences between rough from Venezuela, South Africa, and Russia. By way of contrast, there are innumerable articles and books, as well as collections of photographs, on the differences between Burmese and Siamese rubies, on Colombian and Brazilian emeralds and, finally, on the differences between Ceylonese, Burmese, and Thai sapphires.

One reason for this lack of literature on diamonds may be De Beers' reluctance to tell the general diamond-dealing public where diamonds are coming from. My guess is that De Beers does not want to reveal just how large a proportion of diamonds currently being mined are coming from the Soviet Union.

Since World War II, the Soviet Union has had an enormous hunger for hard Western currencies with which to buy machinery and other Western necessities that have often been keyed to Soviet economic health. It is well known, for example, that the Russians have mined gold in such unappealing locales as Siberia. The cost of production has not really entered into Soviet calculations. In other words, when gold was $35 an ounce the Soviets were willing to pay $70 for labor costs in order to build up a gold nest egg. This could then be used when crops were poor for the purchase of wheat from the West and to hide the generally poor agricultural planning from Soviet citizens. Because of the secrecy surrounding most Soviet internal economic depart-

The De Beers Diamond Syndicate 63

ments, the Russians have been able to hide both their inventory of precious metals and their cost factors.

In the 1950s and early 1960s, the Soviets undertook an extensive geological survey, locating several major diamond pipes in Eastern Russia, the largest of these being the MIR (peace) diamond pipe—a fabulously rich find. At first, rather than deal with the rightist regime of South Africa, the Russians hoped to set up their own marketing operations and sell diamonds directly to the Western diamond cutters and to large-scale users. In point of fact, such an ambitious program might not be beyond Soviet marketing capability, as the Russians do have great banking and financial skills (witness their effective marketing of gold through reciprocal arrangements with large European banks).

However, after several years of attempting to sell diamonds on the free market, the Russians decided to enter into a ten-year agreement with De Beers. In the diamond world, most people say that this proves the Soviets were unable to operate without De Beers, indicating just how powerful the De

The cutting wheel. Diamonds are faceted on these high-speed wheels. The wheels are coated with diamond dust as only diamond can cut diamond. Photo: N.W. Ayres.

Beers people are. Whether this is so remains to be seen. Russian diamond production reportedly has increased greatly over the life of this contract, and indeed, the Russians have attempted to set up a cutting industry, which would add greatly to the value of their rough.

The ten-year contract period has almost ended, and what happens next is uncertain. The Russians have all the ingredients and trained personnel to set up an indigenous cutting and ring-mounting operation. It is not improbable, therefore, that we may see large-scale exports of finished diamond ring production emanating from the Soviet Union that will be marketed throughout the world.

Even if the Russians do not decide to develop their own cutting and exporting of finished diamond products, the problem will still remain as to what they plan to do with ever-increasing amounts of diamond rough. For the moment, there are quite a few diamond dealers going to Moscow and obtaining fairly large parcels of rough. Similarly, there are stories of Russians setting up skeletal offices in New York and Antwerp as possible future outlets for their diamond rough.

My personal belief is that the diamond syndicate will again triumph in its negotiations with the Russians. First of all, they will threaten to make it most uncomfortable for people who will deal in Russian stones. Second, they will offer the Russians a great financial incentive to sign another ten-year contract.

Future Price of Diamonds

The price of diamonds is truly controlled and stabilized by the economic strategy of the De Beers syndicate. Each sight that occurs, ten times a year in London, parcels out only the amount of rough that the diamond syndicate feels can be absorbed by the world market without lowering existing prices. The De Beers syndicate goes further than merely restricting supply, however. They have also made a major effort to create international demand. This has been done through radio and TV advertising. De Beers advertisements of a sophisticated institutional nature are seen in almost every country.

More importantly, De Beers has a way of saturating every possible future market. For example, when it became obvious that Japan potentially represented a large future consumer of diamonds, De Beers made a huge investment in educating the Japanese consciousness to the beauty of gems. Rather than wait for the Japanese demand to develop slowly, the De Beers people staged a saturation advertising campaign throughout Japan, with the ultimate aim of creating overnight a diamond-conscious people.

It is, however, interesting to note that De Beers did *not* change its system of distribution. In other words, the company did not approach one of the financially strong Japanese trading companies, such as Itoh, Mitsubishi, or Mitsui, and offer to ship them large amounts of rough so that they could set up their own cutting operations because they would be more aware of their local Japanese diamond needs. Rather, De Beers continued to ship stones to the traditional diamond-cutting centers in New York and Antwerp, as well as to Israel. Japanese diamond dealers scurried around the world in a frenzied attempt to buy enough diamonds quickly enough and to bring them back to Japan, often charging two or three times their original cost.

The De Beers company has always preferred to be the party that calls the financial tune.

In the early 1970s, the Japanese became the third largest diamond user in the world, following the United States and Germany. However, the oil-induced recession of 1973–74 was responsible for some bankruptcies of major jewelry companies in Tokyo and Osaka, resulting in tens of millions of dollars in lost sales. Many diamond dealers in New York found themselves unpaid for the diamonds they had shipped to Japan.

Although the Japanese had to drop out of the world market for diamonds to a great degree by the latter part of 1974, world diamond sales of the De Beers company did not decline greatly for 1974, as compared with the previous year.

In 1973, total De Beers sales were $1.33 billion, as opposed to $1.25 billion in 1974. This 6 percent drop is not extraordinary and represents proof that De Beers still retains the ability, on a worldwide basis, to stimulate diamond demand even during inflationary and uncertain economic times.

Price increases have varied according to size and quality of diamonds. An interesting fact emerges: the price of D color (the finest color) flawless one carat stones has risen from $1,475 in 1970 to $6,500, wholesale in 1976. At the same time, a 7 point diamond, that is to say, diamonds that are 1/15th of a carat or about the size of a period on this page, have risen less by comparison. They were $250 in 1968, and the price has risen to $400 in 1975. The lesson is clear: the larger and finer the stone, the greater its potential as an investment.

IX

Other Gemstones

It used to be that ruby, sapphire, emerald, and diamonds were referred to by the trade as precious stones while all the other gemstones, such as tourmaline, topaz, quartz, peridot, zircon, opal, garnet, etc., were called semiprecious stones. The Gemological Institute of America has strongly objected to this term. Generally speaking, these other stones have been much less expensive than ruby, sapphire, emerald, or diamonds. However, there has been a tremendous explosion of interest in these stones over the past ten years and fine specimens of the rough crystal groups and the cut varieties of these stones have risen dramatically.

In the $5,000 "Other Gems" portfolio I suggest that fine quality specimen crystal groups with a mounting can be purchased. Very often you can see a lovely, massive uncut tourmaline from Maine or an amethyst crystal group from Brazil. Buying crystal group specimens is a very difficult thing. The piece should have balance as well as good color and a certain amount of dramatic aesthetic appeal. Generally, what looks most beautiful is the best investment.

Similarly, cut specimens (for example, aquamarine) that today will sell for $200 to $400 per carat in the top-quality blue color are probably an excellent investment. Five years ago, the price of top-quality aquamarine was $50 per carat. Similarly, chrome tourmaline, which costs one quarter the price of green tourmaline, is an excellent investment.

Green grossularite garnet—called tsavorite—has been discovered and is selling for prices upwards of $1,000 per carat, but it still can be purchased for investment. Orange grossularite garnet, at $250 per carat, is also a lovely and dramatic-looking stone.

In general, the best way to enter the investment field, as far as these stones are concerned, is to go to the hobby shops and spend a good deal of time window-shopping. As the prices are lower here, one can assemble a large number of specimens for a modest investment.

X

Gem Appraisals for Owners and Estate Trustees

Two important concerns of the potential gem investor are how much the stone he is considering is worth and how much he will be paid for it when he decides to resell. In economics, the ease with which one can sell a stock or bond or any other investment is referred to as "liquidity." One of the reasons that the American stock market has remained so powerful is that if one wanted to sell, say, $30 million worth of IBM stock in a day, it could be done without seriously adversely affecting the price of IBM shares.

Colored gems and diamonds do not have this kind of liquidity. But the whole point of investing in precious stones is that they are meant to be held over a long period of time. They are an "ace in the hole," not to be used in the opening or even in the middle of a card game, but rather to be held almost to the end, if at all possible.

Suppose you inherit a 3 carat ruby from your grandmother. A visit to the Gemological Institute will immediately ascertain whether the stone is a genuine ruby. You have done your homework and you know your stone's color and possibly its origin. You now think you want to sell the stone.

The next step is to obtain an appraisal. One problem that arises with appraisals is that the appraiser generally asks the purpose of the evaluation. If the stone is being appraised for estate tax purposes, there is likely to be one price; if it is for insurance purposes, a second price. If you are showing the stone to a retailer and say, for example, "What's it worth?," expecting the retailer to purchase the stone, his appraisal will be on a third level. Finally, if you show the stone to an appraiser with a view to buying a matching stone for the same amount of money, it will be yet a fourth figure.

Such a procedure is extremely discouraging to anyone hoping to find the value of his ruby listed daily in the *New York Times*. Take heart. Paintings, antiques, *objets d'art*, and a host of other items suffer from a similar lack of standardized appraising. The trick is to find a reputable, honest dealer or retailer who will be willing to give an accurate estimate of what a stone would cost or fetch in today's market, and who would be likely to submit the highest bid. Armed with a rough idea of these valuations—even though there may be a spread of from 20 to 30 percent between the bid and asked figure estimates—you can properly decide on a course of action: to sell or hold for future sale. An appraiser should be judged as one would judge any professional. Apply the following criteria:

Investigate his technical background. Has he been trained at the Gemological Institute of America or at the American Gem Society—or does he have the "experiential" equivalent of such training? (When a person has looked at gems for many years, the handling of them is often as good as, if not better than, these gemological courses.)

Next, what is the reputation of the appraiser in the jewelry field? Often, your local jeweler can give you information on the character and competence of appraisers in your area.

An appraiser should have either a large stock of colored stones and diamonds or access to them. He can arrive at an infinitely better appraisal if he has comparison stones than if he is working entirely from memory.

Finally, an appraiser should reveal openly and fairly all he knows about the stone in question. His primary responsibility is to the person to whom he is giving the appraisal.

XI

What You Can Learn from Auctions

Auctions are an excellent place to examine and learn more about precious gems. By all means attend them to sharpen your eyes to gem color and obtain some indication of the market value of jewelry and stones. But beware: the major buyers at auctions are usually dealers who either have a specific customer in mind for the gems or who want to complete the layout of a bracelet or necklace. They are willing and able to bid higher for the piece than the average layman.

The principal auction houses are Christie's, a publicly traded company listed on the London Stock Exchange, and Sotheby (Parke-Bernet), originally a British auction house. Together they bring in a total of well over $250 million a year in fine art and gems.

Although there is a mystique surrounding the major auction houses (the clerks generally have British accents, for example), you *are* welcome. For a few days before a sale, prospective buyers may examine the rings and other pieces of jewelry to be offered at the sale. The auction houses have developed a high level of expertise in evaluating what is suitable for auction and in which market the auction should take place. For example, Sotheby Parke-Bernet may advise a client to sell a ring in New York, London, Geneva, or in other cities throughout the world.

Briefly, the conduct of an auction follows this pattern: the auction house accepts a ring from a client, places it in an auction, and prints a catalogue for that sale. About one month before the auction, these catalogues are sent out to the mailing list. The description of the ring might read something like this.

Lot No. 58. Sapphire and diamond ring, van Cleef & Arpels. Platinum mounting set with 30 round diamonds weighing approx. 3.25 cts., centering a cushion-shaped sapphire weighing approx. 12.50 cts.

estimated selling price: $25,000

The description would normally be accompanied by a life-size photograph of the ring. If the stone is an important one, the picture might be in color. Do not expect information on the quality of the stone or its origins. It is seldom given.

The estimated value of the above piece—$25,000—is what the Sotheby Parke-Bernet experts think it should fetch in normal times at an open auction.

At the same time, the seller of the ring may place a "reserve" price of, say, $15,000 on the piece. This means that if no one in the hall bids more than $15,000, the auction house will buy it back on behalf of the consignor.

The commission for selling gems at Sotheby Parke-Bernet is 12½ percent for individual lots over $15,000; 15 percent for individual lots of from $5,000 to $15,000; 20 percent for individual lots of from $1,000 to $5,000; and 25 percent for lots below $1,000. Christie's commission is 10 percent.

Generally speaking, the auction houses try to have their estimates match what they think the piece should bring. It seems to me that they have a good record of accuracy in the field of pricing jewelry.

Finally, in all auctions of any kind, in any city, and at any time there is the distinct danger that several dealers will pair together to buy as a group and thus avoid truly competing against each other. This has the effect of keeping the price artificially low, leaving dealers free, at a later time, to

Seven round, brilliant cut diamonds. The most popular shape of diamond is the R.B.C. diamond. Each stone has fifty-eight facets, cut with mathematical precision to yield maximum optical brilliance.

Photograph by N. W. Ayres

This round, brilliant cut diamond is proportionately cut. One can see both the dispersion (the splitting into colors of the white light reflected from the stone) and the brilliance (the sparkle, or return of white light).

Photograph by N. W. Ayres

Two shots of De Beers mining areas. By mechanizing almost all phases of production, diamond-mining costs have been effectively controlled. 4.5 tons of rock have to be mined in order to yield 1 carat of gem diamond.

Photographs by N. W. Ayres

Above Diamond miners at work in South Africa.

Below Diamonds adhere to grease. Rocks with diamond crystals are poured on the grease. These rocks are then jetted with water, leaving only the diamonds sticking to the grease table.

Photographs by N. W. Ayres

The heart of the De Beers system of "sights" is the careful sorting into four thousand grades (by color, clarity, and size) of rough diamond crystals. Note: Some diamond piles are yellowish.

Photograph by N. W. Ayres

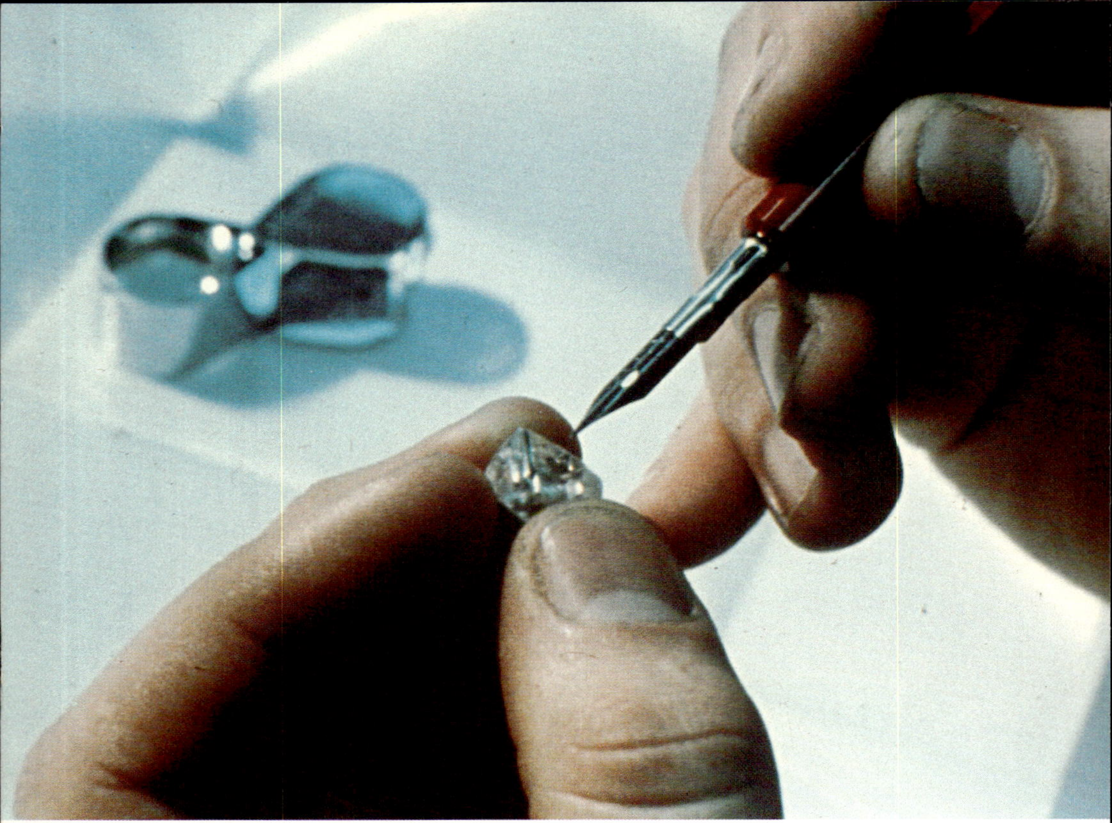

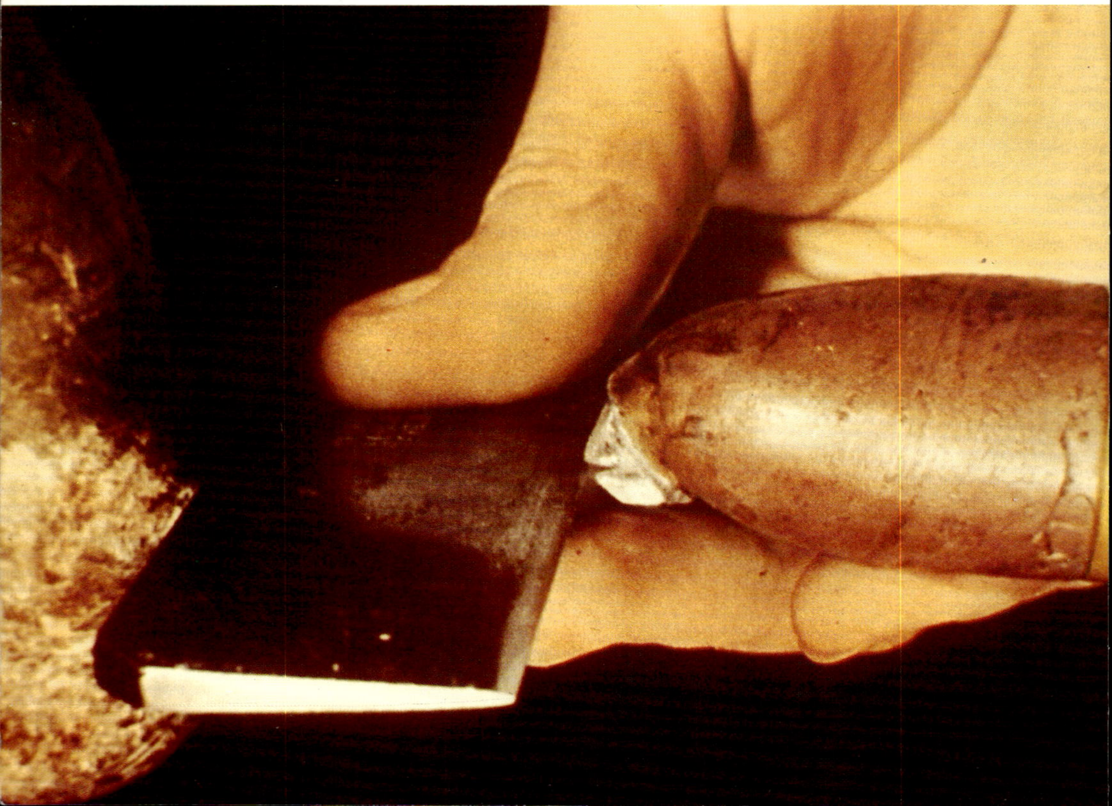

Above A skilled Antwerp diamond cutter examining a stone to check its polish.
Below Fred Claar "louping" or examining a diamond in order to grade it.
Photographs courtesy of Fred Claar, Claar Bros.

Opposite page The diamond crystal rough is marked carefully with India ink and then is expertly cleaved. A mistake can indeed shatter the stone.
Photographs by N. W. Ayres

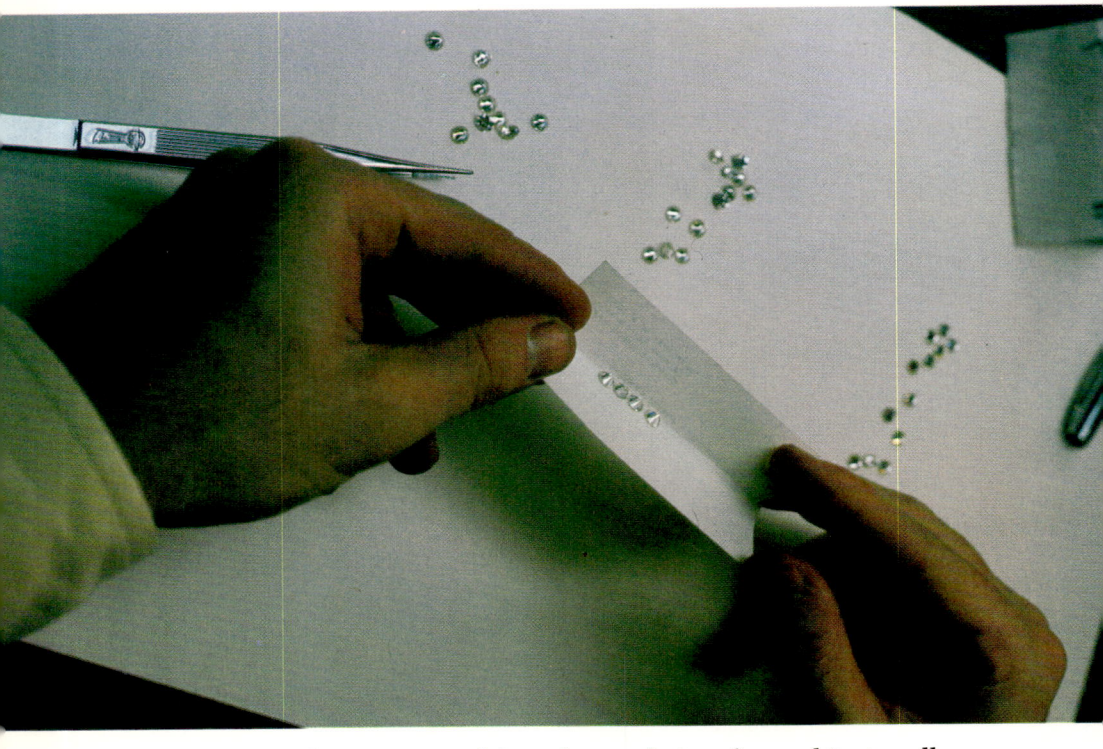

Diamonds are examined for color gradations from white to yellow by laying them top down (table down) in a paper. They are normally graded by comparing one to another.

Photograph by Fred Claar, Claar Bros.

maneuver among themselves and decide who should get the stone and at what price. In the trade this is called the "knockout."

The investor wishing to buy or sell precious stones through an auction would do well to seek the advice of a dealer. This advice on such points as quality and market value is generally worth the price of the dealer's commission—usually 5 to 10 percent. Our firm, as well as most traditional firms, will provide this service.

An examination of past years' auction catalogues reveals an incredible rise in prices. In 1972, for example, the Enid Haupt emerald, a 34.30 carat deep green stone, was sold at auction in New York City for $385,000. Four years earlier this stone had sold for 40 percent less. Today, it is estimated in the trade that this same stone might fetch close to $750,000, a rise of 300 percent since 1968. In 1971, at a Sotheby Parke-Bernet auction, a 44 carat sapphire sold for $60,000. Three years later, a stone of similar quality and size was sold for $200,000.

XII

Investment Portfolio: Gems for $5,000, $20,000, $100,000, and $1,000,000

$5,000 Investment Portfolio

RUBY

For $5,000 one can buy a 1 carat Burmese ruby relatively free of silk. The stone should be brilliant and can be cut in an oval, cushion, or round shape. Any of these shapes are acceptable. *Or* a 2–3 carat Thai ruby. This is a more brilliant stone and it can be larger than the Burmese stone, *Or* a 2–3 carat Ceylon ruby. This will be slightly pinkish. It can be cut in any shape—round, oval, or cushion. The origin of a colored stone is not as important as the quality of the stone.

SAPPHIRE

A 2 carat Ceylon sapphire sells for $1,500 to $2,500 per carat and can be purchased relatively free of silk. *Or* a 1–2 carat Burmese stone for $5,000. This will be deeper in color and less brilliant. *Or* a 3–4 carat very fine Thai sapphire, brilliant, but a darker blue shade.

EMERALD

From .8–2 carat stone. A $5,000 stone can be bluish green or yellowish green Colombian material. This stone

Investment Portfolio 75

will not be flawless; however, it should have a good deal of brilliance and have consistent color throughout. Inclusions in emeralds (as well as in rubies and sapphires) are unavoidable.

DIAMOND

A 1 carat D, E, or F color flawless stone can be purchased for approximately $7,000 to $8,000. This stone has appreciated threefold in the past five years. It should be accompanied by a certificate from the G.I.A. stating its color and flawlessness.

OTHER GEMS

Fine quality specimen crystal groups with a mounting stand can be purchased from the following materials: tourmaline from Maine, either limpid blue (not the dark variety) or yellow green; amethyst quartz from Brazil (difficult to tell if it has been artificially treated); pyrite from Elba, Italy; rose quartz from Arkansas; as well as several others. There should be a contrast between the different colors of specimens. The crystal groups should have a sense of dramatic-looking brilliance. The specimens should be carefully stored away from the dust inside a cabinet.

GEM CUT STONES

Tourmaline from Maine offers a wide range of colors to the collector-investor. Blue, yellowish green, red, and purplish red are colors much sought after. 5–10 carat sizes can be purchased for $100 per carat; thus a collection of ten 5 carat stones can be formed for $5,000.

CUT GARNETS—RHODOLITE GARNETS

Grossularite garnets and almandite garnets can be purchased for between $50 to $100 per carat. If purchased in a clear uniform color, free from invisible inclusions, $5,000 will buy a magnificently integrated collection of garnets.

$20,000 *Investment Portfolio*

RUBY

A 2 carat Burma stone, fine color, little silk. *Or* a 4–5 carat Ceylon ruby, very brilliant, pinkish. *Or* a 4 carat Thai ruby, slightly purplish, should be relatively clean of internal inclusions.

SAPPHIRE

Kashmir is almost unobtainable, but a 2–3 carat stone, if it has a good color, is always a good buy. *Or* Burma sapphire 3 carat stone with no silk visible through the table. *Or* Thai sapphire, 5 carat, relatively free of inclusions and very brilliant.

EMERALD

2 carat stone, Colombian origin. Good color, not flawless. Flawless material is nonexistent. Can be bluish green or any shade of green, but should be lively.

DIAMOND

2 carat D, E, or F color, flawless. Should be accompanied by a certificate from the G.I.A.

CRYSTAL GROUP GEM SPECIMEN

One can sometimes see massive crystal groups of gem quality. These have increased dramatically as museums are big buyers of such crystal groups. *Or* malachite, tourmaline, topaz, peridot, and kunzite are good gem specimens. *Or* other cut colored stones. I would recommend that for the $20,000 investor four groups of $5,000 cut stone portfolios be established in the quartz, tourmaline, beryl, and topaz family of minerals.

$100,000 *Investment Portfolio*

RUBY

4–6 carat Burma ruby, top color, little silk on table. This stone should be of museum caliber. *Or* Thai material, 6–10 carat, almost flawless. Color not purple red. *Or* Ceylon origin, 6–8 carat, not too pink, little silk.

SAPPHIRE

Can be from Kashmir, Burma, or Ceylon, 5–10 carat stone should be very lightly included, if at all.

EMERALD

4–6 carat emerald. It is better to get a 6 carat lightly flawed stone than a larger size with heavy inclusions. Color is all-important.

DIAMOND

5–7 carat D, or E, or F color flawless stone. Round shape is better, preferably cut close to ideal proportions.

For a large investment of $100,000 I recommend the above four stones and not the so-called newcomers, although the newcomers, such as tourmaline and topaz, have shown explosive price rises in the last twenty years.

Rubies, sapphires, emeralds, and diamonds have historically—for the past thousand years—been investment vehicles. Therefore, I would advise sticking to them when considering a large purchase.

$1,000,000 *Investment Portfolio—or How to Set Up Your Own Gem Museum*

If you happen to have a million dollars that you don't know how to use, I think the best thing would be to form a museum collection of precious gems from all around the world. About seventy years ago, J. P. Morgan did just that. He was offered a collection as a block by Mr. Kunz of Tiffany & Co. Morgan bought these gems and gave them outright to the American Museum of Natural History in New York City.

It's not too late today to consider the formation of a similar collection. Such a dream collection might contain fine cut sapphires from Ceylon, Burma, Kashmir (India), Thailand, Australia, and Cambodia. Similarly, one could have fine cut emeralds from Colombia, Brazil, Rhodesia, Tanzania, and Pakistan. Finally, it might contain fine cut rubies from Burma, Ceylon, Thailand, Kenya, Cambodia, and Afghanistan.

Diamonds could be displayed under a microscope, which would be visible from a special opening in a glass case. Various shapes of diamond rough crystals from South Africa as well as from Russia could be displayed. Large specimens of topaz, tourmaline, quartz, and many other stones, along with pictures of the mining areas and the cut varieties of those stones, could be assembled. Commercial as well as specimen quality could be collected and displayed.

There is no question that there is considerable interest in the environment today. Precious stones, which are among the most beautiful things that exist in nature, serve as a reminder to all of us of how beautiful the earth can be. With tens of thousands of young people interested in "rocks," such a museum would be a welcome addition to any community.

What would be necessary, and most desirable, would be to combine fabulous examples of gems at their best with the less beautiful, but equally important, geologic crystal specimens.

Once such a collection is assembled by an investor, many institutions could be prevailed upon to accept and display it.

Appendix 1

Current Prices of Rubies, Sapphires, Emeralds, and Diamonds

Table 1
CURRENT PRICES OF COLORED STONES AND DIAMONDS
OF FINE QUALITY PER CARAT PRICES
(*all prices are in U.S. dollars*)

Carats	Ruby		Sapphire		Emerald		Diamond	
	BURMA	SIAM	GEM	COMMER-CIAL	GEM	COMMER-CIAL	D FLAW-LESS	COMMER-CIAL
1	$ 4,000	$ 500	$1,500	$ 400	$ 6,000	$2,500	$6,500	$1,300
2	5,000	1,000	1,700	600	9,000	3,000	11,000	1,800
3	9,000	2,500	1,900	800	12,000	3,500	14,000	2,500
4	10,000	3,000	2,600	1,000	13,000	4,500	16,000	3,000
5	18,000	4,500	3,000	1,200	14,000	5,000	18,500	3,500
6	25,000	5,500	3,200	1,300	15,000	5,400	18,500	3,600
7	30,000	6,500	3,400	1,400	16,000	5,800	18,500	3,700
8	36,000*	7,500	3,600	1,600	19,000	6,200	19,000	3,800
9	45,000*	9,000	4,000	1,800	22,000	6,600	19,100	3,900
10	50,000*	10,000	5,000	2,000	25,000	7,000	20,000	4,000

* Almost unobtainable

Table 2
History of Diamond Prices

(These prices are for internally and externally flawless diamonds of D color, in a round brilliant cut diamond.)

	Weight in Carats	Value per Carat	Total for Diamond
1968	3	$ 3,000	$ 9,000
1970	3	4,000	12,000
1972	3	5,000	15,000
1974	3	11,000	33,000
1976	3	14,000	42,000
1968	2	2,000	4,000
1970	2	3,000	6,000
1972	2	3,500	7,000
1974	2	8,000	16,000
1976	2	11,000	22,000
1968	1	1,400	1,400
1970	1	1,500	1,500
1972	1	1,900	1,900
1974	1	5,000	5,000
1976	1	6,500	6,500
1968	1/2	700	350
1970	1/2	800	400
1972	1/2	900	450
1974	1/2	1,300	650
1976	1/2	1,500	750
1968	1/10	275	28
1970	1/10	300	30
1972	1/10	340	34
1974	1/10	400	40
1976	1/10	420	42

Table 3
MEDIUM QUALITY DIAMOND—SLIGHTLY FLAWED
(VVS, J COLOR)

	Weight in Carats	Value per Carat	Total for Diamond
1968	3	$1,000	$3,000
1970	3	1,250	3,750
1972	3	1,500	4,500
1974	3	2,700	8,100
1976	3	3,000	9,000
1968	2	950	1,900
1970	2	1,150	2,300
1972	2	1,400	2,800
1974	2	2,300	4,600
1976	2	2,500	5,000
1968	1	550	550
1970	1	700	700
1972	1	900	900
1974	1	1,400	1,400
1976	1	1,500	1,500

Appendix 2

Learning about Gems— A Visit to Gem Museums

The American Museum of Natural History, New York City

One day, while I was sitting in my office, a most extraordinary thing happened. A man came to show us some sapphires, among which was a lovely, deep color blue star sapphire estimated at roughly 94 carats in size. Most star sapphires come from Ceylon and are quite gray in color. Often the star pattern—which may be seen if there is a direct overhead light source, and which is due to internal crisscrossing rutile needles within the stone—is not too distinct. In the case of this stone, however, the color was truly extraordinary and the star was excellent.

I considered this star sapphire to be far superior in color to the famous Star of India, which can be seen at the American Museum of Natural History in New York. It is ironic that the most famous colored stone in the United States became famous after Murph the Surf had stolen it in 1963.

The dealer who was offering this star sapphire was clearly aware that we were most interested in the stone. So, using the same technique that Marco Polo used, he immediately tried to sell us the other stones he had with him. After protracted negotiations, we bought some of the other sapphires. We then began discussing the price for the 94 carat star, which was presented in a ring setting and had come from an estate.

What intrigued me was the fact that this was one of the few times in years of looking at gems that I had seen a stone that I believed to be far superior to a museum-quality piece.

The gem world in New York conducts business at a much quicker pace than in the Far East, where there is a long period of beginning offer, counteroffer, etc. I had a feeling that if we did not put in a strong bid for this stone, the man would take it to another dealer who would purchase it immediately. I experienced excitement and trepidation. Was this stone really superior to the Star of India? The price asked for it was extremely high by trade standards, and if it was not of museum quality, it was no bargain. We also believed that the stone had changed hands several times among New York City dealers before arriving at our office.

The shade of the color of this blue star sapphire was a very deep and rich blue—much more reminiscent of the Burmese shade of color than the Ceylon shade. In the gem world, when one is shown a stone like this, the seller generally claims the stone to be of Burmese origin, while the buyer generally claims that he believes the stone is from Ceylon. The appellation "Burma Origin" generally connotes a finer color stone. The very top color grade for a sapphire is the so-called Kashmir color, which is a rich and deep velvety cornflower blue. The stone need not have been mined in Kashmir, as those mines only yielded stones from 1860 to 1920. Occasionally a Burmese sapphire will exhibit this Kashmir shade of color, but it is extremely rare for a Ceylon sapphire to reach this fantastically delicate hue.

We decided to take a chance and purchase the sapphire on the spot, along with the other sapphires. There were two choices once the transaction was completed. One was to show the stone in the marketplace and try to sell it immediately at a small profit; the alternative—most appealing to me—was to go to the museum and check if the stone was of such high quality.

I called Dr. Vincent Manson, curator of the gem collection, Department of Mineralogy, of the American Museum of Natural History in New York City, and told him I believed I had a stone that was superior to the Star of India.

He replied enthusiastically, "Well, Mr. Zucker, if you would like to show it to me now, I would like to see it."

I went to the museum the same day with my sister. Before going to Dr. Manson's office, we stopped at the gem case that contained the Star of India. At that time (before the Guggenheim Pavilion of Gems was opened at the Museum) the gem case for star stones contained three important gems: the Star of India; the Midnight star sapphire, a purplish mauve-colored sapphire; and the exquisite 100 carat star ruby called the DeLong Star Ruby.

Nearly every school class in the New York City public and private school system is taken to the Museum of Natural History to see these famous gems, among other exhibits. Many years before, when I was ten years old, I too had visited the J. P. Morgan Collection of Precious Stones.

On the day we were to show the star sapphire to Dr. Manson, there was a group of schoolchildren around the museum case. I removed the 94 carat star sapphire from my pocket and casually asked one of the schoolgirls which stone she preferred—this 94 carat stone or the Star of India. She replied, "That one is blue, mister, and the Star of India isn't." It seemed very clear to me that our sapphire was far superior and fit extremely well with the three stones already in the museum collection.

Dr. Manson was thrilled to see the gem. He called it extraordinary and asked about the price. I politely declined to give a price quotation but said that I would be interested in having the stone displayed at the museum for a certain length of time since I felt that it was an aesthetic complement to the J. P. Morgan Collection. I mentioned that our office thought it was definitely a gem of Burmese origin and wanted to know what he thought. He put the gem under a microscope and fiddled around awhile with the dials. Suddenly he cried out with joy: "Look at that!"

Dr. Manson is one of the most highly respected mineralogists in the world today, and he has done a great deal of work on tiny inclusions within gems. Under his 100-power microscope one could see a tiny crack that looked almost like a little hole in a piece of glass with shatter marks about it. This, Dr. Manson explained, was a zircon crystal imbedded within the sapphire. Mystery of mysteries, if this zircon crystal did not have a circle of light around it (a radioactive halo), the stone was presumed to be of Burmese origin. After sighting several other minute crystal inclusions, Dr. Manson told us that he believed the stone was of Burmese origin.

The Museum decided to accept this fabulous gem on loan and it may now be seen in the gem case directly alongside the Star of India.

The Smithsonian Institution, Washington, D. C.

In the Smithsonian Institution, Dr. Paul Desautels has expertly and tastefully arranged various stones which serve to demonstrate the shades of green found in emeralds. The "Spanish Inquisition" necklace has many emeralds dating back to the original pre-Colombian mines in South America. The stones are a deep velvety green and are smoothed and rounded but not faceted. They were probably mounted in this necklace at least three hundred years ago.

A few feet away, in another case, is a 38 carat emerald, again of a matchless color—this time faceted precisely into an emerald-cut form. This stone also offers an example of how faceting can enhance the brilliance of a stone, bringing out all the nuances.

The Smithsonian also houses several large sapphires, for example, the 423 carat Logan Sapphire and the 198 carat Bismarck Sapphire, two stones that display very fine shades of blue sapphires.

There are quite a number of extraordinary diamonds in the Smithsonian, among them the dazzling Hope Diamond with its sapphire blueness. The Hope Diamond can now be traced back to one of the stones that Tavernier brought from India and presented to Louis XIV of France.

The Bank Melli, Teheran, Iran

While it is somewhat impractical to consider going to Teheran to see gems, there is no question that their collection of colored stones and diamonds is the finest in the world today. These gems were primarily a part of the ancient Indian collections of precious stones. In 1739 the Nadir Shah, a Persian ruler, captured and sacked the city of Delhi. Delhi had been ruled by a long line of Mongol leaders who placed a great value on gems. The Nadir Shah took the booty back to his capital city, Meshed, Persia. The treasure moved around a great deal throughout Persia and even through Afghanistan. People lost their lives trying to retain these gems.

In the late nineteenth century, Nasir Ud-Din Shah opened a museum in the Golestan Palace, where he planned to show his gems to traveling guests. Finally, in 1938 the gems were made part of the National Bank of Iran—an extremely important fact in gem history, as these gems today are collateral against the currency notes issued by the Iranian government, and are valued at $3.5 billion.

In 1960, the gems were placed on exhibit in the national bank, the Bank Melli, in tastefully lit cavernous vaults. The arrangement was done by Boucheron of Paris, one of the finest gem retailers in the world.

Because the gems are collateral, the Shah of Iran has taken great pains to make them accessible to his people as well as to tourists, with a view to bolstering confidence in the fiscal integrity of his government. In addition, the Irani collection represents a link with all parts of Asia. The diamonds, for example, came from the Golconda Mines in India, the same mines that yielded the fine stones that Tavernier, the gem merchant, wrote about in his *Six Voyages of Jean-Baptiste Tavernier*. Fabulous rubies from distant Burma and remarkable spinels from Ceylon are also part of this collection.

Two cases in the Bank Melli are devoted to emeralds. One

contains a box of cut emeralds, mostly cabochon. It had been believed that the finest emeralds from Colombia were taken back to Spain and Portugal by the conquistadores. However, upon seeing these boxes of emeralds in the Bank Melli, one realizes the correctness of Tavernier's assertion that the finest emeralds of Colombia were sent to the Philippines, where they were sold to the Indian maharajahs.

Why is this so? After all, one would think that the first duty of the Spanish explorers would have been to return the finest gems to their motherland. The fact is, however, that then as now gems are most highly esteemed in the East, where they command extravagantly high prices. It is therefore not surprising that in the long run these stones seem to flow from West to East.

In the Iranian collection, one sees emeralds of incredible quality scattered almost helter-skelter among the cases. A 100 carat deep blue green cabochon rests in a tray with about two hundred cabochons ranging in size from 20 to 100 carats. These stones were the cream of the Muzo, Colombia, (velvety yellowish green mine quality), as well as diggings from the El Chivor mine, which are a deep blue green color.

Also in the Iranian collection are swords embedded with large emeralds bearing inscriptions lauding Persian rulers. There is one belt buckle composed entirely of Burmese rubies, eighty-four in number. The large 11 carat stones are of the finest pigeon blood color.

This Irani gem collection was enlarged in the eighteenth and nineteenth centuries to include examples of European workmanship. Some fine, naturally yellow South African diamonds which were cut on the palace grounds in the late 1800s are exhibited. It is interesting to note than the Irani sensibility preferred naturally colored yellow diamonds over flawless white diamonds. While there are some white diamonds of very large size in the collection, these were part of the original Indian treasure trove seized by the Nadir Shah, cut in the old Mongol style—very flat top and only one series of step cuts on the crown.

In visiting museums, of course, it is well to remember

Somerset Maugham's dictum that after one hour one's eyes get tired, and it is probably better to visit a museum often and for shorter periods of time than to race through and see a great deal with exhausted eyes.

Appendix 3
The Gemological Institute of America

The Gemological Institute of America was founded by Robert Shipley with its parent office in Los Angeles. Mr. Shipley's dream was to have the Institute launched on a firm scientific foundation. The late Dr. Edward Wigglesworth of the Boston Society of Natural History wrote the first G.I.A. colored stone course.

An educational institution where one could take courses utilizing microscope techniques and study precious stones was created. In addition, the G.I.A. offered a professional gem analysis and testing service to both the jewelry trade and private individuals. Because it was during the Depression, and because, in fact, there were very few scientifically trained people involved in the jewelry trade, the Institute got off to a slow start. However, under the guidance of Richard T. Liddicoat, Jr., director (in Los Angeles), Robert Crowningshield (who heads the New York City office), and Bert Krashes, the Institute has grown in importance each year. It is a nonprofit organization which sponsors both correspondence courses and a six-month in-residence program in gemology that can lead to a graduate gemology diploma. (Eunice Miles is the educational adviser to contact in New York.) Approximately 350 Americans hold its graduate gemologist diploma.

Appendix

In addition to these lengthy courses, shorter one-week classes are offered in diamond appraisal, colored stone identification, jewelry designing, jewelry repair and stone setting, etc. Anyone with a week to spare and about $255 can learn to distinguish between a genuine topaz and a glass imitation, between a naturally colored diamond and one that has been treated to induce color, or to recognize a diamond that has ben treated with laser beams.

The G.I.A. has perfected the use of a spectroscope to test for the identity as well as the origin of color in certain precious stones, although the courses employ the microscope as the primary diagnostic instrument.

In both California and New York, the G.I.A. maintains large gem trade laboratories where excellent gemologists write reports on diamonds and colored stones which have been submitted to them. A real breakthrough came when the G.I.A. succeeded in establishing an extremely accurate system of grading both the color and clarity of diamonds. The best color of diamond, which is a truly colorless white diamond, is called a D color diamond. An E or an F color is also a white diamond, but it is less white than the D color. After F, the colors descend from G to Z, with the bottom range being extremely yellowish. The letters J to K show a trace of yellow in a face-up position, which can be seen even by the untrained eye.

The diamond is also inspected with 10-power magnification and is examined for internal flaws, fractures, inclusions, presence of black "carbon spots" (rare), and so on. If the stone is flawless under 10x, it is so graded on the report. If it has flaws, depending on how close to the center of the stone the flaws are and their seriousness, the stone can be graded as follows:

Flawless Complete absence of internal or external flaws or faults of any description when graded under 10x binocular magnification.

Internally flawless A complete absence of internal flaws or faults, but with minor identifying surface characteristics such as growth lines, small naturals, or extra facets.

VVS 1–2 Minute inclusions such as a feather or pinpoint that are seen with difficulty even by the trained eye under 10x.

VS Small inclusions that neither affect the appearance or durability of the diamond and cannot be seen with the unaided eye.

SI Fairly obvious inclusions under 10x magnification with the lower end of this grade containing stones in which the flaws may be visible to the unaided eye when observed through the back of the stone, but not in a face-up position.

Imperfect Those diamonds in which flaws can be seen with the unaided eye and are serious enough to lower the durability of the stone.

The nature of the inclusions found in a diamond is fascinating; more than twenty different minerals have been identified as crystals in diamond, including diamond itself, garnet, and peridot. As a matter of fact, the study of these inclusions is the basis for learning a great deal more about how, when, and where diamonds were first formed in nature.

Stones will often be sold with the agreement that if a certificate from the G.I.A. is not issued, the sale may be cancelled or the stone's price reduced. I suggest that people buying very fine diamonds today ask for accompanying certificates stating the color and clarity classification for the particular stone in question. The cost for a report on a carat stone is $30; the cost on a 10 carat stone, $136.

A number of years back, many diamond dealers objected strenuously to being told by these "scientists" what a diamond color or quality was ascertained to be. However, with the passage of time, even these traditional diamond merchants accept and appreciate the G.I.A. certificates. As a result, the work of the G.I.A. laboratory is very much in demand. This service has brought the G.I.A. a great amount of prestige, and has established worldwide respect for their diamond-grading integrity.

The system of grading abroad depends upon the country. In France, for example, there is much less standardization of classification grades. A certificate may be issued on the basis of what can be seen through a 2-power loupe, a 6-power loupe, and a 10-power loupe. Similarly, in Belgium and in the Far East there is no gemological institute of the size of the G.I.A. Therefore, one can see why at some point the important diamonds from any cutting center or any precious gem-trading center eventually find their way to the G.I.A. for grading and certification.

In the colored stone field, because of the innumerable shades of color—the myriad tints of red, the large number of delicate shadings of green, and the many nuances and degrees of blue—the G.I.A. has been unable thus far to set up a color standard for rubies, emeralds, and sapphires. However, this is a subject which is getting the increasing attention and effort of the G.I.A. staff, and it will not be surprising if a workable system emerges in the near future. The Institute will issue a certificate as to whether a stone is a genuine ruby, emerald, or sapphire, a synthetic stone, or glass.

Rabbi Nahman of Braslov, one of the great Hasidic rabbis and storytellers, once said, "God never repeats himself." Nothing in nature, including people, is the same as anything else. There is always a difference, however slight it may be. After all, why do the same thing twice? This is one of the factors that make gems so fascinating. For each is an individual with characteristics which make it at least slightly different from any other gem. An Indian merchant I once met claimed he could remember every ruby and sapphire over one carat he had examined—and he had seen many!

In addition to visiting museums, reading gem books, and going to pre-auction sale exhibitions, anyone interested in diamonds and colored gems would do well to take an introductory course at the Gemological Institute in New York or Los Angeles. It need not be a six-month course—even a week-long class would provide a very good start to an appreciation and understanding of these extremely fine and unique precious stones.

Appendix 4

The Evolution of Jewelry and Cutting Techniques

Since Biblical times, there has been a slow but constant evolution in emphasis from the style and workmanship of the jewelry mounting to the stone itself. Archaeologists have discovered beautiful emerald necklaces from the early dynasties of Egypt. Although the settings are designed in a spectacularly simple manner, the emeralds themselves are generally of a poor quality and unfaceted. The gold workmanship, though, is of the highest standards.

Similarly, if we visit the Metropolitan Museum of Art in New York and see the fabulous Morgan collection of Medieval and Renaissance jewelry, we can appreciate the extraordinary workmanship of European jewelry makers. The finest artists of the Renaissance had a much stricter period of apprenticeship than a painter has today. Ghiberti, for example, began as a goldsmith in the fourteenth century and only later became a painter. Botticelli, a consummate painter, was also trained as a sculptor and goldsmith. The result of this interdisciplinary training was that jewelry was sculpted, crafted, and finished in an artistic and meticulous fashion.

In examining a boat-shaped pendant from the Venetian school of craftsmen of the sixteenth century in the Morgan collection, we can see that the pendant, perhaps six inches

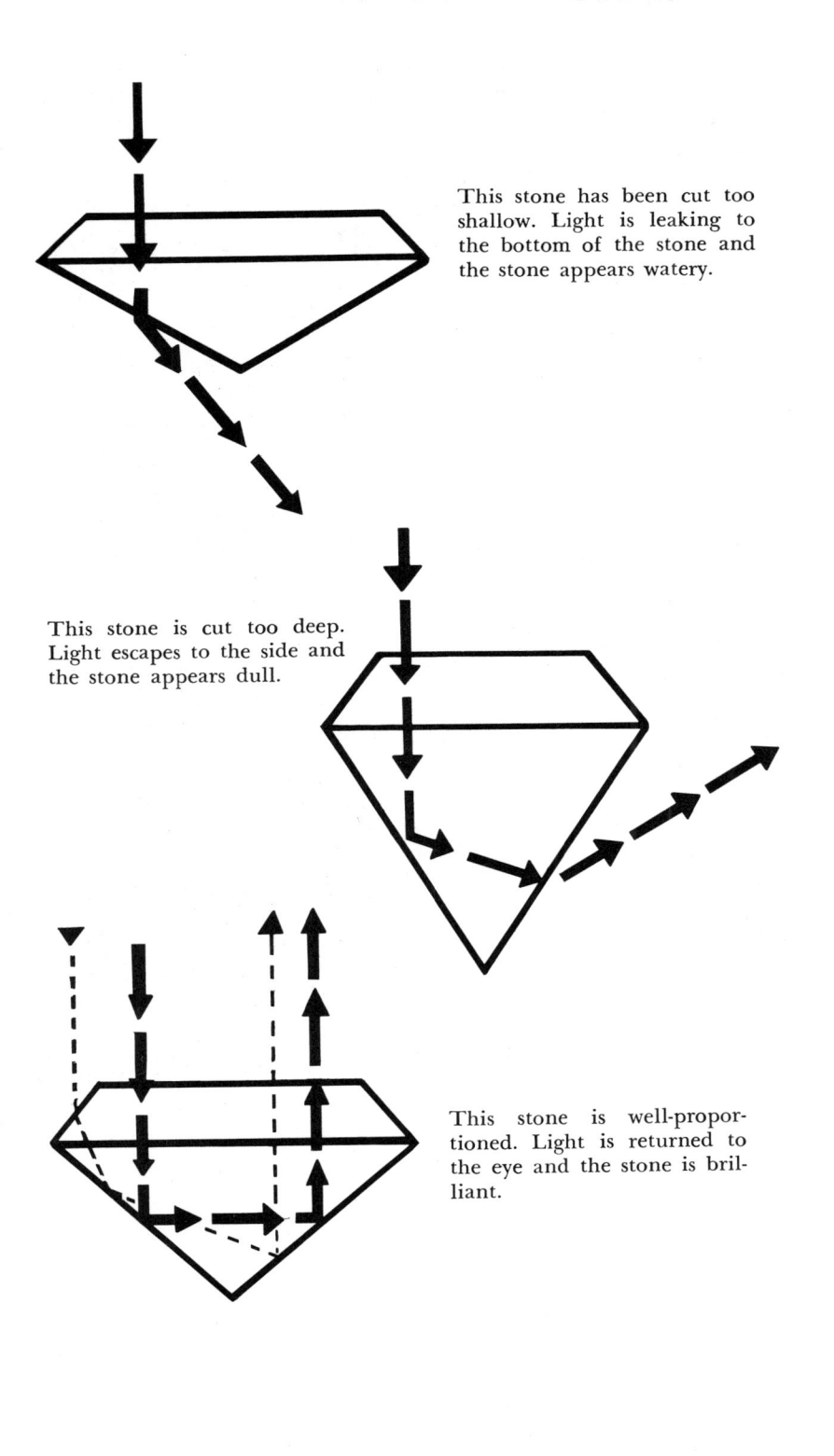

This stone has been cut too shallow. Light is leaking to the bottom of the stone and the stone appears watery.

This stone is cut too deep. Light escapes to the side and the stone appears dull.

This stone is well-proportioned. Light is returned to the eye and the stone is brilliant.

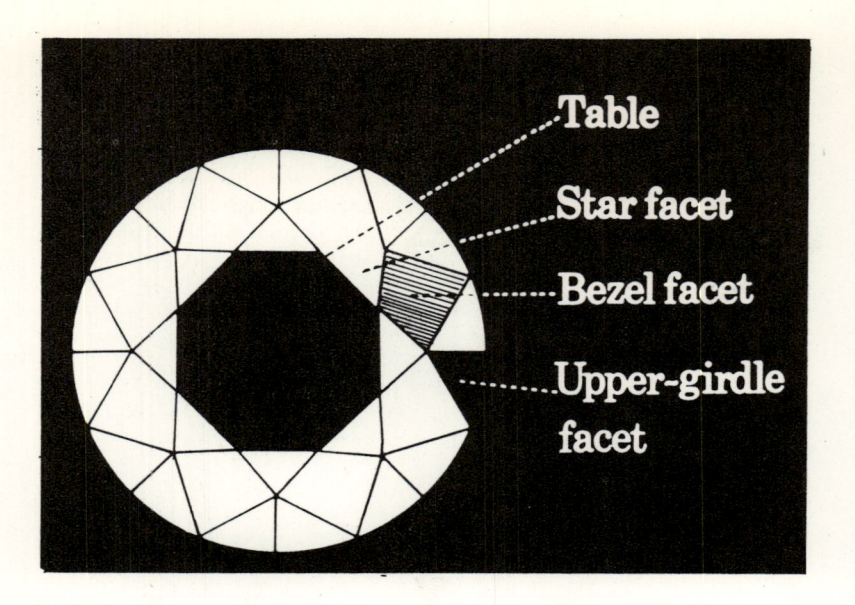

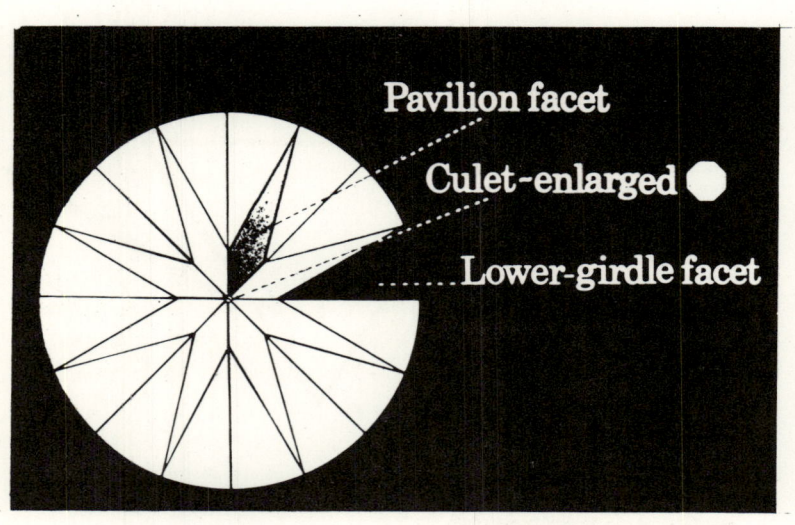

The parts of a diamond.

high, is an exact-scale reproduction of a Venetian trading ship. The sails are of finely worked gold, the bow of the ship is enameled, and natural pearls dangle playfully from the bow. Colored stones (rubies, sapphires, and emeralds) mined in India and in remote Burma stud the edges of the deck. These colored stones, however, were chosen primarily for their color. The style of cutting was *en cabochon*—having a rounded top. If such a stone was faceted, the faceting was crude—*en table*—with only one rudimentary, flat surface. Occasionally one sees a flattish-top stone, also called the "table" cut. But stones were primarily cut and set for color, exhibiting little brilliance.

The enameling was a very slow process. If any faults remained through the final enameling, continuous buffing of the enamel would remove these imperfections on the surface, and the piece might be reenameled to give a more perfect top layer of enamel.

The piece would often be built around a natural pearl of fairly large size. Sometimes the pearl served as a dangling portion to the "boat," or it might serve as the torso of a mermaid or sea triton. These pendants were highly imitative of nature, with movable parts that would swing when they were worn.

It is a testimony to the high degree of craftsmanship that went into these pieces that their worth today far exceeds the value of the individual stones making up the pieces. In a recent European auction, for example, a ship pendant fetched upwards of $60,000.

In the 1640s, stones were cut in "sixteen facets." What this means is that diamonds, then coming in increasing numbers from India and Brazil, could be cut and faceted to unlock the brilliance within the stone. Light could enter the stone and, as a result of the phenomena of optical reflection and refraction, could emerge and "sparkle."

Investors generally are more concerned today about the quality and color of the stones. A piece that is not quite so ornate but has a fine quality stone or stones may command a greater price at auction than a Renaissance "work of art."

The prices of raw materials for ring mountings—gold,

silver, and platinum—have soared recently. The movement of gold from $35 an ounce to $150–$200 an ounce has not substantially increased the value of any mounting. A rough rule of thumb for any fine piece of jewelry in the $5,000 to $10,000 range is that the mounting costs between 10 and 20 percent of the value of the whole piece. The remaining value is accounted for by the stones themselves. Gold and silver have had a continuous, more or less equal relationship over many centuries.

The United States fixed the ratio between gold and silver at 16 to 1 for quite a few years around the turn of the century. More recently, however, silver has declined substantially vis-à-vis gold. Platinum has always been a rare metal, and with any minor increase in demand, prices for platinum have moved upward very sharply. Silver has tended to sell over the last few years at $4 to $5 an ounce, platinum at $150 an ounce, and gold from $150 to $200 an ounce.

Gold may be used in different degrees of fineness, expressed as fractions of purity—24 carat gold, for example, being completely pure, 18 carat gold less pure, and 14 carat gold still less so. Absolutely pure gold, without the addition of any alloy, does not have sufficient hardness to be an effective jewelry metal—so that some amount of debasement—an addition of an alloy—must be employed. It is essential that 18 carat gold or better be used in any piece of jewelry. The 14 carat variety seems to be gaining popularity in the United States, but 18 carat gold remains most popular in Europe.

It seems very foolish to me to spend thousands of dollars on a fine stone and mounting, and then to save a few dollars by using 14 carat instead of 18 carat gold. This lessens the value of the ring at a European or a Far Eastern auction.

Gold can be yellow or white. I regard white gold, however, as a substitute metal and advise against its use. White gold does not have the strength of platinum and is used because it is cheaper than platinum.

There are general styles and theories of the use of yellow gold or white platinum in the mounting of the ruby, emerald, sapphire, and diamond. Historically, it has been

Appendix

fashionable to use yellow gold for rubies, as yellow is considered a more flattering color alongside the red ruby. Emeralds, with their softer nature, have usually been set with gold prongs, although these, in turn, can be soldered onto platinum or yellow gold. In the case of sapphires, it has been more common to use platinum—and yet it is quite permissible, even stylish, to use yellow gold.

Appendix 5
The History of Fabergé: The Ultimate Craftsman

The mounting of jewelry is the art of placing a gem within a setting that will enhance the inherent qualities of the stone itself. The current feeling is that the gem should count for the major part of the value, with the setting secondary. I consider this a terribly cold-blooded approach. Just as one would not think of framing a fabulous Rembrandt painting in a plexiglass frame, so, too, one should try to choose a proper setting for a gem. If the setting is a beautiful one, there is always the chance that the piece as a unit—gem plus setting—will be regarded as a work of art and be worth much more than its constituent parts would bring separately.

Fine mounting of jewelry is never a matter of luck. It is always the result of long years of training and extremely careful preparation.

The greatest jewelry craftsman of the nineteenth century was Fabergé, a French Huguenot whose ancestors had left France because of the persecution of the Protestants. They settled in Russia, and Fabergé became the court jeweler to the czars. Fabergé, a most remarkable man, wanted to assemble a group of international jewelry experts, true specialists in their fields. He hired Finns, Letts, Slavs, Hungarians, Frenchmen, and Italians, and provided them with luxurious quarters in St. Petersburg and Moscow.

Appendix

The late 1800s in Russia saw the greatest concentration of wealth in the fewest hands. Russia was industrializing rapidly. Because there was no middle class, the money flowed directly to the czars. Once Fabergé gained the confidence of the ruling class, cost was no object in the production of fine jewelry.

Fabergé set up a factory in Moscow that employed seven hundred workers, each with his own workbench, each working on clocks, watches, rings, brooches, necklaces, or small fantasy objects of exquisite art. Some craftsmen would prepare designs for these pieces and others would execute them. Fabergé himself did not work on any of the pieces, although he purchased the colored stones and diamonds to be used. He roamed through the factory of his seven hundred craftsmen and peered over their shoulders. If a piece did not meet his most exacting standards, he would take the hammer he carried at all times and smash the piece. This system, which does not seem to be in accord with modern psychological techniques of support and encouragement, nevertheless produced incredibly perfect jewelry.

The height of Fabergé's art is represented by his famous Easter egg presents, created each year for the Czar and the Czarina. Easter in Russia has always been a very special time. It is both a celebration of the coming of spring and a religious holiday—almost a melding of Christmas and Easter into one. On a piece of gold and finely powdered, perfectly formed colored enamel, Fabergé's workmen would encrust rubies, sapphires, emeralds, and diamonds, creating an egg two inches to ten inches high. This egg opened, and from within might come a rooster or other animal that sang a tune or made various motions. All these movable parts would be created by Fabergé's expert watchmakers.

A few of these eggs have been sold at auction over the years—with a recent sale bringing $260,000 at a Geneva auction. The stones within these Fabergé pieces of art are not extraordinary, although they are perfectly matched. But there is no doubt that Fabergé kept alive for future generations standards of workmanship that go back through the Italian Renaissance to ancient cultures.

Appendix 6

Two Men Who Preferred Gems to Paper Money and the Stock Market: Marco Polo and Louis XIV

Marco Polo

Marco Polo is probably the most famous gem dealer of all time. While he was growing up in Italy, his father, Nicolo Polo, and his uncle, Maffeo Polo, decided that there were more opportunities in Constantinople in the precious ruby, sapphire, and emerald trade than in their native Venice.

The Polo family, accordingly, left their beloved Venice in the early part of the thirteenth century and went to Constantinople. After several years there, upon hearing reports of the fabulous wealth of the Tartar and Mongol kingdoms, they decided to travel to the East, with the idea of both buying and selling gems in that barely known kingdom of Cathay. It took them three years to reach the court of Kubla Khan—the voyage was considered so dangerous that the Polos were afraid to bring Marco along.

In those days, when a gem dealer traveled and arrived in a large community, on the first day of his stay he would

Appendix

present a few of his finest gems as a gift to the monarch. This gift would show him to be a man of discriminating taste and a welcome addition to the community. He would then be a guest of the monarch until he left. On the last day of his stay in that town or kingdom, the monarch, in order to show the gem dealer what a beautiful and gracious ruler he was, would give some gems as a gift to the trader.

By giving and receiving gifts, the Polos thus wended their way across the Persian Empire, through the Gobi Desert, until they came to the court of Kubla Khan. After receiving their precious stones, Kubla Khan was entranced with the Polos. They were probably the first Europeans to visit the East. Kubla Khan was a man who combined extraordinary military ruthlessness with a great sense of aesthetics and intellectual curiosity. When he found out that there was such a thing as Christianity, and an institution such as the papacy in Rome, he asked the Polos to return to Rome and bring back a hundred monks with whom he could have a discussion about the true nature of Christian belief.

He gave the Polos beautiful Chinese gems of sumptuous turquoise and jade, as well as rubies mined in Burma and delicate sapphires from the far-away island of Ceylon. With these gifts the Polos returned to Rome.

The Pope was at that time involved in his own pressing political problems, and while he did not want to pass up this opportunity to make contact with the great Kubla Khan, he somehow could not spare the resources to do so. He consequently hit upon a compromise—a few rugs, a small assortment of Venetian jewelry, and two priests.

The Polos decided to take Marco on this long, arduous trip back to the kingdom of Kubla Khan. Although the two priests had been prepared for the rigors of the voyage by the Polo brothers' stories, when the trip became difficult, outside of Tabriz, Persia, the priests deserted the Polo family and ran for their lives back to Rome.

More valuable than any rugs, than any Venetian works of art, the Polo brothers brought one great treasure to Kubla Khan: the terrific storytelling skill of young Marco Polo. When Marco Polo arrived at the court of Kubla Khan, he was nineteen years old. Kubla Khan was so taken with Marco's ability as a storyteller—his vivid descriptions of the cities in which he had lived as a boy, Venice, Genoa, other trading cities on the Mediterranean—that he made Marco Polo his official ambassador to many parts of his kingdom.

Marco Polo would visit and trade in gems in the various cities of Kubla Khan's empire. He would then return to the court and describe in great detail to Kubla Khan how the people lived, what they thought of the Mongolian rulers, what their beliefs were, and what they treasured and hoped for.

The Polo family wanted to return to Italy, but Kubla Khan was so enchanted with his ambassador that for seventeen years he denied them permission to return home. There were very few Mongol rulers in comparison with the numbers of people they had conquered throughout the Eastern world. With a force of less than a million people, they managed to subjugate hundreds of millions of people from China to Persia, India, and Russia.

As mentioned in chapter one, Marco Polo was amazed to discover that the Mongols had developed the first paper currency in the world. This consisted of a scrap of rice paper with rudimentary block printing on it; it was countersigned by six Mongol generals. The punishment for counterfeiting was death. The volume of paper currency was quite large, and it was accepted throughout the Mongolian empire.

Marco Polo himself would generally barter gold for gems or gems for gems. The idea of people having faith in a scrap of paper, of turning over a beautiful, rare, irreplaceable gem for a man-made scrap of rice paper, seemed miraculous to him. Marco himself put little trust in this form of currency, and his reluctance and fears for the future of this paper currency, which he expressed to Kubla Khan, later turned out to be true. When hard times came to China several hundred years later, there was a runaway inflationary period; paper currency was discontinued by the Ming Dynasty in the fifteenth century.

Shortly before Kubla Khan died, Marco Polo and his family were permitted to return to Italy. Upon their return to Venice, Marco Polo's stories about Kubla Khan and the empires of the East were at first derided by his fellow Venetians. Marco was called "Il Milione" because he never could tell a story about the East without saying that they had a million talents of gold, or a million people built a city, etc.

The Polos invited the cream of Venetian society to a banquet at which Marco first regaled the skeptical audience with stories of Kubla Khan. Dressed as they were in the rough sheepskins of the Mongolian nomadic tribes, a quaint, otherworldly quality clung to their stories. The Venetians were not believers, however. It was only when the Polos ripped out the linings of their jackets and hundreds of beautiful gems, which they had bought during their long stay in the East, came rolling onto the ground that these stories were accepted and treasured by the Venetians. With this combination of great experience and great wealth, the Polos became one of the leading families of Venice.

Shortly after this dinner, Genoa went to war against Venice. Marco Polo, who was the commander of a ship, was captured by the Genoese. He was thrown into jail for a year with a Genoese writer, Rusticello, who wrote down all of Marco Polo's adventures. These now form the kernel of "The Travels of Marco Polo," for many hundreds of years the most widely told adventure drama among the European peoples.

Louis XIV of France—The Sun King

Another connoisseur of fine gemstones who was also offered the possibility of paper money was King Louis XIV of France. In the 1600s, his court at Versailles was known as a place where one could see truly fabulous rubies from Burma, sapphires from Ceylon, and diamonds from India.

The Sun King had many theories about how to live a civilized life. He had fairy tales read to him each night, never ate less than a twelve-course meal on gold plates, and felt that rubies, sapphires, and emeralds, because of their lovely colors, were appropriate for daytime wear. Colorless diamonds would only be donned at night, when their "fire" and brilliance could add magic to his candlelit ballrooms.

An extraordinary thing happened to the Sun King late in his reign. A Scotsman named John Law (who had studied finance in Amsterdam and gambling in Venice) proposed to King Louis XIV that he issue paper money. I would suppose that after having spent his lifetime amongst the material, real world of brocades, rugs, tapestries, colored stones, diamonds, and silver and gold coins, Louis XIV thought this novel idea extremely bizarre. To ask a French subject to accept a piece of paper in exchange for tangible gold or silver coin seemed too ridiculous for words to Louis, and he flatly refused.

After the death of Louis XIV, John Law had greater success with the Duke of Orleans, the regent of France. The new government of France accepted John Law's proposal and the Scotsman became the most influential economist of his time. Money was printed and accepted and a great prosperity held sway in France in the mid-eighteenth century.

However, much like developments in our time, the French government secretly began to print vast amounts of paper money. Gradually, a discount was established between the worth of paper money and gold and silver coinage. At this point John Law formulated his second great innovation—the flotation of a huge stock issue. With the court's approval, he issued stock in a new company called the Mississippi Company. This company held the rights to develop the vast Louisiana territory in the western part of North America, as well as parts of India and the Far East.

John Law had engravings printed showing the cliffs of Louisiana covered with emeralds! People were anxious to get rid of their devalued paper money and used it to buy shares of Mississippi Company stock. Prices boomed on the stock exchange. Mississippi Company stock offered at 400 French livres rose to 18,000 livres within three years' time. During this period, the word "millionaire" first came into use.

The government printed and loaned more and more money to sustain and fuel this speculation. Prices for food, rent,

Appendix

and clothing increased astronomically. Paper money again started to sell at a discount to gold and silver coinage. Suddenly the stock market started to weaken and completely collapsed within a year. John Law fled to Venice and died penniless. Throughout this monumental collapse of the French economy, silver and gold coinage maintained its value, as did ruby, sapphire, emerald, and diamond jewelry. This collapse so seriously weakened France that economic historians point to it as a causal factor of the French Revolution of 1789.

Glossary

Alluvial deposit. Debris and gems carried by a river; found along a riverbank
Brilliance. The return of white light to the eye; the "sparkle" of a precious stone
Carat. 1/5 of a gram; unit of weight
De Beers Syndicate. The so-called diamond syndicate
Diamond. Carbon arranged in an isometric way
Dispersion. The splitting of white light into various colors. When a diamond is turned, you can see the play of colors because of this optical phenomenon
Gemstone. It has beauty, rarity, and portability
G.I.A. The Gemological Institute of America—a nonprofit, educational institute
Inclusion. The internal landscape of a gem
Kimberlite. The veins containing diamonds
Melee. Tiny precious stones less than .5 carat size. The bulk of diamonds and colored stones are "melee size"
Reflection. The return of light to the eye after it passes through the gemstone
Refraction. The bending of light within a stone
Rough. Uncut gem material; cut and faceted rough is a gem
Ruby. Corundum that is red
Sapphire. Corundum that is blue or any color other than red
Sight. The parcel containing rough stones sent ten times a year to two hundred fifty diamond dealers

Silk. Inclusions of rutile that are interwoven and look like silk

Spinel. A gem, often red or blue, which can resemble a ruby

Synthetic Stones. Having the same physical and chemical proportions as gems but man-made and of limited commercial value

Bibliography

Background Studies

The following books cover the history of jewelry from earliest times to the present day.

Jewelry Through the Ages, by Gregor Gregoretti (New York: McGraw-Hill, 1970). Translated from the Italian, this book is sumptuously illustrated and presents an extensive history of gem cutting and the use of precious stones in jewelry. It is also a marvelously documented study of the major pieces of jewelry to be found in the principal museums and collections throughout the world.

The Great Book of Jewels, by E. and J. Heiniger (Greenwich, Conn.: New York Graphic Society, 1974). This book is a study of the stones themselves and presents the gemological data on precious stones. Because of the size of the illustrations and the care taken in presenting them, it is a most remarkable study of the principal gems of the world.

The Story of Jewelry, by J. Anderson Black (New York: William Morrow & Co., 1974). An informative, precisely written British treatment of the gem world, this book also contains a history of jewelry from prehistoric times and is perhaps the best study of the current and possible future trends in modern jewelry.

Jewelry from the Renaissance to Art Nouveau, by Claude Fregnac (New York: Octopus Books, Ltd., 1973). Although this is a very short book, it is clearly written and covers the highlights of style changes in jewelry in the last few hundred years.

The Art of Jewelry, by Graham Hughes (New York: Viking Press, 1972). This book contains excellent chapters that give detailed descriptions of how gold and silver are crafted.

Gemological Texts

There have been several major studies of the methods of testing colored stones and diamonds published by the Gemological Institute of America. *Handbook of Gem Identification*, by R. T. Liddicoat, Jr. (Los Angeles Gemological Institute of America, 1969) is considered the standard text. Similarly, B. W. Anderson's *Gem Testing* (London: Butterworth, Ltd. 1971) is an excellent standard British work. And, finally, R. Webster's *Gems—Their Sources, Descriptions, and Identification* (New York: Anchor Books, 1970) is another respected study.

Of a more technical nature: E. J. Gubelin's *The Internal World of Gemstones* (Zurich: ABC Edition, 1974). This is a standard text on gem inclusions, i.e., what the inclusions within a gemstone can teach us. Dr. Gubelin is a most remarkable man—a gem merchant, scholar, and photographer. This book is extraordinarily beautiful.

Pierres précieuses dans le monde, by Henri-Jean Schubnel (Paris: Horizons de France, 1972). This book is another excellent photographic study of gem inclusions as well as a fine review of the history of precious stones.

Museum Collection Studies

Paul Desautels has written a fine study, *Gems in the Smithsonian Museum* (Washington, D.C.: Smithsonian Institution Press, 1972). He has also written a most exciting text on minerals as well as precious gems, *The Mineral Kingdom* (New York: Grosset & Dunlap, 1974).

Bibliography

The Crown Jewels of Iran, by V. B. Meen and A. D. Tushingham (University of Toronto, 1968). This book is a landmark study of the difficulties the authors encountered in examining the fabulous Irani collection, as well as a most detailed study, with color illustrations, of the splendors of the collection. An extraordinary book.

A study in Russian and English of the gems in the Soviet Union, which is historically quite accurate, is *Precious Stones in Russian Jewelry Art in the XII to XVIII Centuries,* by M. V. Martynova (Moscow: Iskusstuo Publishing Co., 1973).

Books by Gem Dealers

There have been some books written by gem dealers that give a feeling of the profession. Lewis Kornitzer's *The Jeweled Trail* (New York: Sheridan House, 1941) is a lively study of how Mr. Kornitzer learned the gem trade and what the 1920s and 1930s were like among gem dealers in Europe.

Historical Studies

Of interest to the more specialized reader is *The Cheapside Horde,* by R. Wheeler (London: Lancaster House, 1928). This is a study of a sixteenth century gem dealer's stock that disappeared in an apparent cave-in, only to be unearthed three hundred years later. It makes fascinating reading.

G. D. Goitein's *Letters from Indian Merchants* (Berkeley: University of California, 1974) consists of a series of letters which were written by Jewish pearl and stone dealers who traveled to India in the eleventh century. Their correspondence with relatives and fellow stone dealers in Cairo proves that things have not changed too much in the gem-trading world in the last thousand years.

History of Diamond Production and the Diamond Trade, by Godelhard Lenzen (London: Barrie & Jenkins, 1970). This is a most thorough review of the history of diamonds throughout the world. It is an unparalled, detailed study of the ups and downs in the pricing of diamonds in the past.

Popular Magazines and Gemological Studies

The Gemological Institute of America publishes a quarterly, *Gems & Gemology*, containing many fine articles of a technical nature on gems.

The *Jewelers Circular Keystone Magazine*, published monthly, is a readable, business-oriented review of events within the jewelry business in the United States.

Lapidary Journal (P.O. Box 2369, San Diego, Cal.) is a monthly magazine for rock hounds and lapidary enthusiasts.

The National Jeweler is a retail, jeweler-oriented magazine that specializes in trade gossip and is an excellent source for finding jobs in the jewelry business.

Acknowledgments

No book is written in a vacuum. I would like to deeply thank the following: My remarkable father, Charles Zucker, who from the beginning advised me to write this book. I thank Luzer Kaufman for his encouragement and enthusiasm. The rest of the New York office: Willie Rosenfeld, Sang Sup Hahn, Bob Simmons, and Bernie Grosz, as well as Bertha, Cipora, Rachel, and Chumie, have aided greatly. Abroad: Kan Yue's confidence has meant a great deal to me. The help of Victor Klagsbald and Benek Borger was invaluable. Here in the gemological world: Bob Crowningshield, Bert Krashes, Eunice Miles, and my mentor Cap Beesley have all been untiring in their help.

Photographically, John Cubito, Peter Schaaf, and Reid Rutherford have enriched the text with their beautiful work.

Dr. Vincent Manson's advice has been most useful. The manuscript was excellently prepared by Marion Lister. The world of gems has been clarified in my discussions with my friends: Milton Moses Ginsberg, Michael and Elizabeth Varet, the other Bernie Zucker, Jeanne and Alfred Moldovan, Bob and B. B. Gray, Bill and Libby Reilly, and John Flattau. Tom Powers urged me to start. Sam Beizer aided on many technical jewelry fine points. My fellow colored stone dealers have been uniformly helpful, as have so many others in the diamond world. I thank Jan Mitchell for his artistic advice and Rosser Reeves for his help. I am indebted to Lotty Zucker, Nikki Zucker, as well as to Margot Zucker Mindich and Lenny Mindich for their support and suggestions. Sheri Safran's work as my agent is what enabled this book to see the light of day. Rachel is a gem, and finally, to that most beautiful of storytellers, Diane, I give my thanks.

Index

Advisory fee, 23, 25
Afghanistan, 16, 33, 78, 87
Alexander, Mr., 27
American Gem Society, 70
American Museum of Natural History, 78, 83–86
Amethyst, 67, 75
Appraisals, 69–70
 See also Prices of gems; and value of under specific types of gems
Aquamarine, 67
Auctions, 71–73
Australia, 26, 78
Austria, 33

Barnato, Barney, 47–48
Beads, 9–11
Belgium, 93
Berquem, Louis de, 43
Beryl, 77
Bismarck Sapphire, 86
Bombay back, 30
Botswana, 58–59, 60–61
Botticelli, Sandro, 94
Boucheron (gem retailer), 87
Brazil, 14, 36
 amethyst of, 67, 75
 diamonds of, 29, 43–44
 emeralds of, 33, 34–35, 78
Brilliance, 12, 21, 43, 97, 109
Burma
 rubies of, x, 13–15, 16, 19, 87, 88
 sapphires of, 26, 28, 31, 78, 84

Cabochon, 88
Cambodia, 16, 33, 78
Carat, 98, 109
Carnaiba (Brazil), 34–35
Certification of authenticity and quality, 23, 92–93
Ceylon (Sri Lanka), 14, 16, 17, 20, 26–30, 78, 83, 84
Chatham, Caryl, 37
China, x
 paper money in, 3, 105
Chivor (Colombia), 33, 35, 88
Christie's, 40
Cocktail rings, 31
Colombia, ix, 14, 33–35, 38, 78, 88
Color of gems, 11–12
 See also specific types of gems
Corundum, 21, 25, 26, 109
Courses in gemology, 90–91, 93
Crystal groups, 67, 75, 76
Cutting techniques
 Bombay back, 30
 evolution of, 94–99
 See also specific types of gems

De Beers syndicate, 46–62, 63–66, 109
Desautels, Paul, 86
Diamonds, x, 42–66, 109
 brilliance of, 43, 97, 106
 current prices of, 80–82
 De Beers syndicate in, 46–62, 63–66, 109
 dispersion of, 43

G.I.A. grading of, 91–93
history of, 29, 42–44
processing of, 59–62
refractive index of, 21
in sample investment portfolio, 75, 76, 77
Soviet, 62–64
value of, 29, 38, 45, 47, 57–58, 64–66
whiteness of, 12, 30, 88
Dispersion, 43, 109

Egypt, 32, 94
Elba (Italy), 75
El Chivor, *see* Chivor
Emeralds, 32–39, 62, 94
brilliance of, 21
color of, 35–37
current prices of, 80
in museums, 86, 87–88
in sample investment portfolio, 74–75, 76, 77–78
sources of, 32–35
synthetic, 37–38
value of, ix, 29, 38–39, 41, 73
Erickson, Joan, 9–10
Evolution of jewelry and cutting techniques, 94–99
Eye beads, 10–11

Fabergé (jewelry craftsman), 100–1
Fee for advice, 23, 25
Fluorescence tests, 22, 28, 37–38
France, 92–93
paper money in, 3, 5, 106–8

Garnets
grossularite, 68, 75
red, 21
Gemological Institute of America (G.I.A.), 16, 21, 23, 28, 38, 45, 67, 69, 70, 109
description of functions of 90–93
Germany, 65
Ghiberti, Lorenzo, 94
Gilson, Pierre, 37
Glass, 21, 22, 91, 93
Golconda, 43, 87

Gold
carats of, 98
price of, 97–98
white, 98–99
Gubelin, Dr., 28
Gutwirth, Aaron, 53
Gutwirth, Bernard, 53
Gutwirth, Hendrick, 53
Gutwirth, Henri, 53
Gutwirth, Gutman, 51–53

Hong Kong, 23
Hope Diamond, 86

Inca civilization, 32, 33
Inclusion, 109
India, 18, 33, 35, 36, 42, 43–44, 87
Iran, 17, 38, 87–89
Italy, 75

Japan, 65
Jeffrey's rule of squares, 44–45

Kashmir, 26, 28–29, 78, 84
Kaufman, Luzer, 27, 115
Kenya, 14, 16, 20, 78
Kimberly (South Africa) 47–48, 59–60
Kubla Khan, ix, 3, 103–6
Kunz, Mr., 78
Kunzite, 76

Law, John, 3, 106–7
Liquidity, 69
Logan Sapphire, 86
Louis XIV (King of France), x, 3, 106–8

Magical property of gems, 12
Maine, 67, 75
Malachite, 76
Manson, Vincent, 84–86, 115
Maugham, Somerset, 89
Mayan civilization, 32, 33
Melee, 31, 38, 109
Melville, Herman, *Moby Dick*, 12
Metropolitan Museum of Art, 94
Miles, Eunice, 90, 115
MIR diamond pipe, 63

Index

Moghul empire, 17, 33
Mogok (Burma), 13, 14
Morgan, J. P., 78, 85
Mountings, 100
   cost of, 97–98
Murph the Surf, 83
Muzo (Colombia), 33, 35, 88

Nadir Shah, 17, 87, 88
Nahman, Rabbi, 93
Nasir Ud-Din Shah, 87

Oil crisis, 6, 65
Opals, refractive index of, 21
Oppenheimer, Sir Ernest, 49–50
Oppenheimer, Harry, 50, 55, 56
Orapa mines (Botswana), 59, 60
O'Reilly (trader), 46

Pakistan, 78
Paper money, 3–8, 105–8
Peridot, 76
Peruzzi (diamond cutter), 43
Philippines, 33, 88
Platinum, 98–99
Polo, Marco, ix–x, 3, 17, 19, 83, 103–6
Portfolio of gems
   samples of, according to cost, 74–78
   size of, x, 7
Precious stones, definition of, 67
Prices of gems
   at auctions, 72–73
   comparison of, 29–30
   current, 80–82
   increases in, ix, 81–82
   See also value of *under specific types of gems*
Pyrite, 75

Quartz, 76, 78

Reflection, 109
Refraction, 21–22, 109
Refractometer, 21–22
Rhodes, Cecil, 47–48
Rhodesia, 33, 35, 78
Rome, ancient, 32
Rose quartz, 75
Rubies, 13–25, 62, 109
   color of, 15–19, 24, 25
   current prices of, 80
   inside of, 19–20
   mounting of, 25
   in sample investment portfolio, 74, 76, 77, 78
   selling of, 24–25
   sources of, x, 13–15, 23
   synthetic, 20–23
   value of, ix, 20, 23–24, 25, 29, 40
Russia, 33, 35, 62–64, 78, 101
Rutiles, 19, 28–29, 110

Sandawana emeralds, 35
Sapphires, 26–31, 62, 86, 109
   author's story of purchase of famous stone, 83–86
   color of, 11, 26, 84
   current prices of, 80
   in sample investment portfolio, 74, 76, 77, 78
   inside of, 19
   sources of, x, 26–28
   synthetic, 28–29
   value of, 29–30, 31, 40–41
Schubnel, Dr., 28
Semiprecious stones, definition of, 67
Shape of gems, 9–11
Shipley, Robert, 90
Siam, *see* Thailand
"Silk," 19, 28, 110
Silver, price of, 97–98
Smithsonian Institution, 38, 86
Socrates, 18
Sotheby Parke-Bernet, 40, 41, 71–73
South Africa, 46–50, 56, 59–60, 78, 88
Spectroscope, 38, 91
Spinels, 17, 21–22, 87, 110
Sri Lanka, *see* Ceylon
Star of India, 83–86
Stocks, 5–6, 69
Strawberries, 45
Stress lines, 20
Synthetic stones, 110
   See also under specific types of gems

Tanzania, 78
Tavernier, Jean Baptiste, 4, 44, 86, 87, 88
Thailand (Siam), x, 14, 16, 17, 26, 29, 30, 78
Tiffany & Co., 78
Topaz, 76, 77, 78, 91
Tourmaline, 67, 75, 76, 77, 78
Twinning lines, 20

United States, 65
  mining in, 29, 67

Van Gogh, Vincent, 11
Verneuil (ruby-maker), 22

Weight vs. purity, 24
Wigglesworth, Edward, 90

Yogo Gulch (Montana), 29

Zambia, 33
Zircon crystal in sapphire, 86
Zucker, Charles, 47, 115